W9-AZB-329

F*** Leadership

How to Motivate and Mentor
Your Team to True Success

JOhn Maxwel
"21 Irrefutable laws of
leader.

By Josh Coats

Copyright © 2019 Josh Coats

All rights reserved. No part of this book may be used or reproduced in any manner whatsoever without prior written consent of the authors, except as provided by the United States of America copyright law.

Published by Best Seller Publishing®, Pasadena, CA
Best Seller Publishing® is a registered trademark
Printed in the United States of America.

ISBN 9781703349399

This publication is designed to provide accurate and authoritative information with regard to the subject matter covered. It is sold with the understanding that the publisher is not engaged in rendering legal, accounting, or other professional advice. If legal advice or other expert assistance is required, the services of a competent professional should be sought. The opinions expressed by the authors in this book are not endorsed by Best Seller Publishing® and are the sole responsibility of the author rendering the opinion.

For more information, please write:

Best Seller Publishing®
1346 Walnut Street, #205
Pasadena, CA 91106
or call 1(626) 765 9750
Toll Free: 1(844) 850-3500

Visit us online at: www.BestSellerPublishing.org

Contents

Introduction
The Leadership Mind-Set 11

Chapter 1: The Four Ms.. 15
    1. Model... 16
    2. Motivate 16
    3. Mentor 17
    4. Multiply 20
    Doing the Right Thing Well.............................. 21

SECTION ONE
MODEL 23

Chapter 2: Production—Every Leader's
Greatest Responsibility.. 25
    Living Proof.. 26
    You First.. 29
    Expanding Your Reach 31

Chapter 3: PUKE Goals (Urgency) 35
    What Do You REALLY Want?........................... 37
    Urgency Creates Focus 39
    Urgency Breeds Creativity 42
    Urgency Demands Ownership 46
    Own Your Mission... 49

Chapter 4: Leaders Are Listeners 55

Respect Breeds Respect 57

Start with the End 58

The Real Story 60

Global Listening 61

Beautiful Data 64

Chapter 5: Leaders Relate (or Not) 67

Leaders Relate and Duplicate. 67

Outreach by Franchise 68

Relatable and Duplicatable 70

Sustainable 72

SECTION TWO
MOTIVATE 73

Chapter 6: Taking Control 75

We've Only Just Begun 76

Servant Leadership 77

Chapter 7: The Boundaries of Motivate and Mentor 79

Know Your Own Value 80

The 80/20 Rule 81

A Dose of Reality 83

Setting Appropriate Boundaries 85

It's Your Team 86

To Motivate or Mentor? 89

Chapter 8: Law of Energy 93

Making It Work for You 95

Your Best Friend or Your Worst Enemy—You Choose 100

Law of Process 103

Chapter 9: Motivation Made Easy 107

The Coach Also Gets Coached 109

Your Toolbox 111

PUSH Mastermind Game Plan 111

Ordinary Systems Lead to Extraordinary Results 113

SECTION THREE

MENTOR 115

Chapter 10: Work with the Working 117

Four Personality Types 118

Task-Oriented / People-Oriented 123

Filling Your Stadium 129

You've Just Gotta Show up for Practice 132

Chapter 11: The Art of Asking Questions 135

Law of Familiarity 135

Beyond the Story 138

Teaching Them to Fish 140

Chapter 12: Mentoring Made Easy 143

Principles of Mentorship—Implementation 143

Work with the Working 144

Hold Proper Expectations 145

Develop a Specific Game Plan 145

Establish a Way to Track That Plan 146

Tracking the Plan 146

Go Forth, and Mentor 149

SECTION FOUR
MULTIPLY 149

Chapter 13: Empowering Your Leaders 151
    Speaking Up.. 151
    Breaking Out... 153
    Managing Capacity 157
    Spending Time with the Right People............................. 160

Chapter 14: Continual Growth—Additional Streams 163
    Life by Design... 164
    Delegating.. 166
    Leveraging Your Time and Talents 168
    Outsourcing 171
    Life Is More Than Work... 173

About the Author...177

Acknowledgments..179

Author's Note

You want to succeed. You want to reach your goals. Even more, you want to make a difference. You want to inspire others and help them to succeed.

But that takes leadership. And according to what you have seen, heard, and read, that means you have to be a larger-than-life personality. You have to have a celebrity status on social media. You have to be the most organized and structured human on the planet. You have to memorize thirty-seven different personality types and know how to communicate properly with each one.

How in the world can you do that and still find a way to lead by example? Apparently, being a leader is only for superhumans that have some type of natural-born qualities the rest of us just do not possess.

This is what you've grown to believe. That is why your business has become a struggle and a burden instead of a purpose and a passion.

Foreword
by Micah Folsom

7 figure earner, Top 10 in her company in 2014, Top 15 in her company 5 years straight, 6k+ in her down line.

I met Josh over 3 years ago when he was in his first year of trying to get his coaching business up and going. He was in the trenches doing the unsexy hard work and I had already reached the highest rank in our company. I didn't realize he'd bring to the table exactly what I needed at that time to level up even more as a leader and in life.

His background as a John Maxwell coach paired with his no nonsense motivation and mentorship around the most important things helped me create the systems and mindset shifts that were essential in order to continue to create not only the business that I wanted, but more importantly the LIFE that I had been working so hard for.

This book will help anyone, especially in the network marketing industry, set a solid foundation and understand how to be the CEO of their business from day 1 without letting their business completely take over their lives.

We really can have it all and he will help you understand exactly how to have an AND life instead of an OR one.

The principles he teaches are simple and effective and can be applied at any level. If you're a beginner, you'll appreciate the big picture understanding and save yourselves years of missteps that will hopefully streamline your success and save you from years of frustration.

If you've been in the industry for awhile and are feeling stuck or burnt out, the teachings in this book will help give you a fresh perspective to breathe life back into your business and get you excited to show up for what you started.

His firsthand experiences and stories he shares throughout the book had me laughing out loud and make it so easy to understand the concepts he's teaching. (That diva voice though)

Having reached a level of success in my company that only a handful have achieved, I still walked away with so many tangible takeaways that I can implement myself and share with my team.

This is a book you'll want to read multiple times and be sure your teams get their hands on early so they can have the most success possible and find joy in this journey because they're equipped to work smarter, not harder.

Josh, I'm forever grateful for your mentorship and your passion to help entrepreneurs take our lives to the next level. #letspuketogether

-Micah Folsom
@micahfolsomfit on IG
www.micahfolsomfit.com

Introduction

The Leadership Mind-Set

I've mentored thousands of entrepreneurs over the last five years. On call after call, I've found myself talking to people who seem to have this one limiting belief in common: *I don't know if I'm a good-enough leader to* _____
(fill in the blank with whatever goal they're trying to accomplish that includes other people). So many people are confused about what **leadership** really is. This certainly is true in the network-marketing industry, but it applies in any scenario where a person's goals depend on motivating others. Take a stroll through the personal development or business section of any bookstore. You'll find that almost half the books on the shelves deal with leadership. And yet no one seems to understand what leadership is—*what does it really mean to be a leader?*

Like anything else in life, people begin to take book titles (making assumptions about what the books actually say) and create a mental picture of what leadership looks like. They see these books in every airport and Barnes and Noble. They follow on Instagram these people they look up to, seeing their idols dressed perfectly, always smiling and sexy, and always full of energy. And once again, they reinforce that picture in their heads of what a "leader" is.

So, as a member of the John Maxwell Team (John Maxwell is **the** leading authority on leadership), and someone who claims to mentor the top leaders in the network-marketing industry, how *dare* I make a statement like "Eff Leadership"?! These false notions of leadership that people generally carry around in their minds is the kind of "leadership" about which I do dare to make such a statement.

One of the biggest revelations I've had about leadership actually came from a John Maxwell book called *Becoming a Person of Influence*. J Max says that a **true leader** is defined by four stages: *Modeling, Motivating, Mentoring, Duplicating*. (Although I like to change *duplicating* to *multiplying* because Four Ms roll off the tongue more smoothly.)

I would be willing to bet that the picture of a leader you've drawn up in your head is of someone who is good looking, outgoing, very confident, and impressive with words. When you consider the Four Ms, you no doubt already imagine a leader must be a fantastic motivator and mentor. And yet, you've probably never thought of a leader as being the best **modeler**.

This concept absolutely blew my mind! As a motivational speaker myself, I love the motivating and mentoring aspect. It makes me feel powerful. It makes me feel influential. It makes me feel *important*.

But the greatest quality a leader can ever possess is modeling, which is simply leading by example. *True* leaders are gritty, in the trenches, practicing what they preach. They are self-motivated, self-disciplined, and far from perfect because they're still learning and growing themselves, which means they are also failing regularly. And of course, they are *relatable* because of the hustle they are still putting in.

Here's why we overlook the first M: It's not sexy! We *all* want to be on stage. We *all* want to have people listening to our every word. We *all* want to feel like the person who gave someone their "aha" moment. But very few of us want to put in the *work* it takes to earn that trust with others.

I've seen leader after leader lose momentum in their businesses because they modeled only long enough to get people on their side. And then, they turned to "leading" their teams, forgetting all about that crucial first step. They lose that gritty discipline that got them their team to begin with. They slip into "management" mode. Over time, these leaders lose the respect of their teams.

Deep down, the real problem is that many people think leadership is the thing we earn for working hard, the thing that gives us permission to stop working quite so hard and just get others to work hard for us. That's not my idea of leadership! Even with my own PUSH Coach certification I'm currently developing, part of the curriculum will include achieving something *yourself*. The last thing I want is a bunch of underperformers walking around thinking they've earned the right to coach people.

My goal in writing this book is **not** to convince you to stop working on your leadership, but instead to understand that all true leadership starts with *leading yourself*. This book is about breaking through the stereotypes and assumptions in wide circulation about the meaning of leadership, and helping you see the full picture of what a leader really looks like. Then you'll be able to grasp that, truly, anyone can do it— including you!

Leading yourself is the most unsexy thing you could possibly imagine. It comes down to owning your own faults. As Jim Collins says, it is "looking in the mirror for someone to blame and looking out the window for someone to praise (Good to Great)." It is self-discipline and self-motivation.

If you work on yourself continually, you'll find that motivating other people starts to come naturally. People will *want* to hear what

And it can be heartbreaking to see just how few people are actually willing to go through the process with you to get where you are.

A summary follows explaining what you need to do to implement the Four Ms. Afterword, I will use the rest of this book breaking these concepts down to show you how they can work for you and your team, and giving you a simple strategy for implementing each of them.

1.   Model

You have to *show up* each day the way that you want your team to show up. If the end goal is to multiply yourself, remember that it is YOU that is being multiplied in the long run. If you were to multiply—infusing what you're currently doing and achieving into another new person, would that individual be successful? If the answer is no, you have some work to do! Before you can motivate or mentor anyone else, you have to first lead by example. Talking the big talk just isn't enough. No one cares. They can see right through it. People don't do what we say, they do what we do.

2.   Motivate

No strings attached. When motivating others, we have to remove our emotions from the outcome. Too many times we get so emotionally involved with anyone who says yes that we put our hope and our future in their hands. That's not being a leader; that's being a chump! How dare you put the pressure of your life and your goals on someone else? As a motivator, your number one job is to create an environment of belief *for them*, not to use them to find your own belief.

I encourage my clients to think of their team page, message threads, and other motivational tools the same way they think of their social media. If you're doing social media right, you show up every day regardless of engagement. You're constantly studying engagement and algorithms to find out what works best and how to improve the interaction, but you're not, in any way, emotionally attached to any particular individual follower or friend. If anything, you judge yourself based on the performance. But you would never go through and individually judge each person who is or isn't engaging with your posts.

I'm going to tell you something that is going to set you free: *People are flakes and liars.* Just because they said they want to work as hard as you doesn't mean they want to. Just because they said they'd show up doesn't mean they will. So, do you just let people walk all over you? NO! You set proper boundaries that help you understand whether this person is someone who is earning your motivation or mentorship.

Ninety percent of people pay for a motivator only, and yet you're trying to deliver them a mentorship package. Or even worse, you're delivering a motivational package and expecting mentorship results. This will make more sense when you read the next section describing mentorship. But please, quite simply remember this: It is not anyone else's job to hit *your goals.* Your job is to motivate them by giving them an environment and a structure to help them to achieve success *if they decide they actually want to.*

3. Mentor

Numbers don't lie, people do.
... I trust what you can show me.

—Grant Cardone, *Be Obsessed or Be Average*

Work with the working; people have to earn an opportunity for mentorship. My good friends, Robb and Chelsea Pearson, said these magical words from the stage: "Work with the working!" I almost fell out of my seat because it was the first time I'd heard another person in the network-marketing field say something in alignment with what I had started teaching. They had hit the top rank in their company and were speaking from the stage, at an event, on their top tips to do the same—reach the top.

Personally, I love to use my own business structure as an example for others, to help them to see the logic behind my thinking. You see, when dealing with our own situations, we are always emotionally attached, both to the process and the outcome, which makes it almost impossible to see things logically. As my friend Andy likes to say, "Common sense isn't common these days." So, one of my favorite coaching tricks is using analogies from other industries, which my clients aren't emotionally attached to.

As a business coach and trainer, do you think I charge the same amount of money for a group session as I do for a 1:1 session? Do you think that people who pay $200/month for a group training get as much personal access to me as someone who pays me $1000/per hour for personal coaching? Of course not—that would be ridiculous. And yet, one of the complaints I hear the most from people in groups is that they really wished there was more 1:1 access. That's like going to a Tony Robbins event and getting upset that you didn't get to speak to him personally before or after the event to ask your own specific questions. Some of his events cost $25K and still come with no personal access. Why? Because they didn't pay for it.

This is one of the hardest things for me to help my clients understand. As a network marketer, no one actually pays you for any type of training. It's just part of the package that comes with joining your team. You provide training and mentorship. So, you find yourself spending all day and night answering the same questions for the same people who never take the time to look things up for themselves, and who never produce any results because they're too busy asking questions. Please remember these words: The people who deserve your time rarely ask for it. The people who ask for it rarely deserve it.

The solution: *Create packages.* In my training on the John Maxwell Team, something that was talked about a lot was *staying in your lane.* So even though you may not have "packages" for sale like I do, I want you to *think of the Four Ms as lanes.* Knowing which lane you're supposed to be in with each specific person and situation in your business is incredibly important. That's the *number-one reason* I wrote this book: to help you see the lanes clearly so that you can operate in them.

Think of the *effort* people put in as the *price* they're paying for their package. It's not always about results. I hear a lot of leaders say things like, "You can earn a call with me for hitting these specific numbers." Here's the problem with this approach: It looks like it's performance-driven, but really it's not.

Every person on your team has a different level of current potential based on current strengths, momentum, and natural talents. While I do believe in preaching a minimum, the problem with this scenario is it also turns the minimum into a **maximum**. In other words, it doesn't encourage anyone to go beyond the minimum. Personally, I would rather work with an underperformer who shows up for work every day than an average performer who shows up only twice a month.

Too many times, you are working with people who are scoring five points a game, who in reality could be scoring twenty to forty points a game. And you are ignoring people who are showing up for practice every day, just because they haven't scored yet. Well, of course, they haven't scored yet; they are new at this sport and haven't learned how to get in position yet. But if they're shooting the ball over and over, they are likely to start scoring soon, if someone gives them a chance and then continues to challenge them to do so.

But I thought we were supposed to work with our top performers? Isn't that what statistics and leaders have taught us? You have to remember that your industry is different than any other. In other industries, *everyone* shows up every day. They don't have virtual businesses they can hide behind. No surprise, the results usually speak for the effort. But in an online business, you may have several people selling $500/month that would be selling $5,000/month if they just showed up every day.

You also have to remember that you are probably advertising that "anyone can do it, with or without experience. I'll teach you as long as you are willing to put in the work." That means you didn't hire people who were qualified. You recruited people who were willing. So, work with the willing, as long as they are actually *working*. I'll teach you in the mentorship chapters how to pick ***who deserves this*** and who doesn't.

4.   Multiply

This is the easy part. While it's all simple, it's also very difficult. So few people are willing to work hard enough to ever earn your mentorship. And the only way to intentionally multiply is through mentorship. Occasionally, you'll get lucky and multiply on accident. Although the reality of an accidental multiplication in your business is usually just having had the good fortune to find someone willing to work hard, with or without your help.

Finding someone like that is not necessarily the result of the Four Ms. More like the luck of the draw. Don't ever feel bad or guilty about getting one of these gems; we're all praying for them! But don't take too much credit either.

True multiplication is the result of your taking the time to mentor the few who have earned it. Sure, it is frustrating and hard work to get people to that point. Yet once they are at that point, it all becomes super easy. Because multiplying yourself into other hard-working, self-motivated people is just a matter of being intentional about teaching them what you're doing.

Not to undermine or undervalue others, but people don't always think. Most people are followers, and we have to teach them to be leaders. This means that, even if you're showing them everything you're doing, you still have to take the time to turn all of that into a duplicatable system as you explain it to them—walking them through to set it up, and then, holding them accountable to follow through. I'll teach you the systems in my motivate and mentor chapters. You just have to make sure to teach them!

Doing the Right Thing Well

It's that simple. By this point, I'm sure you're seeing that it's not that easy. But it is simple. I'm going to spend the rest of this book teaching you how to more specifically implement each of the Four Ms. I will also address the myths and stereotypes that will arise, blocking the view as they try to hold you back from applying these essential aspects of leadership.

Your limiting beliefs are ever so smart, and they play dirty. They will do everything they can to use your humanity and heart against you. They'll try to blur the lines and suck you into delivering elements of your package to people who haven't paid for your package. That is why I wrote fourteen chapters to help you dissect these principles, implement specific systems, and become the leader you've always dreamed of being.

One more thing! Another beautiful aspect of the Four Ms is that they operate as a grading system. Think of the Four Ms as progressional steps. If you model well enough, you'll acquire plenty of people to begin motivating. If you motivate well, you'll have excited people putting in work that now need to be mentored. And if you're mentoring people, you'll have the ability to multiply yourself into them.

As you read through these chapters, try to determine which step you're stuck on. Remember that doing one step well naturally leads to the next step. For instance, if you find that you have no one to motivate, it's not because you're a bad motivator. It's because you haven't modeled enough to even get to the next step.

Put your focus on the step that would get you where you want to be. If you don't have anyone to motivate, don't worry too much about implementing the mentoring strategies—you're not there yet. Read it, learn it, and put it in your back pocket to save for a later time. *You don't need to do everything well to succeed; you just need to do the right thing well.* And the right thing is *always* implementing the step that will allow you to level up, getting results!

Additionally, I've created some surveys to go along with this content to help you to dig in even deeper to your specific struggles within the Four Ms. You can find these surveys at joshcoats.com/survey. Once you take these surveys, my team will be in touch with some free resources that will help you address your specific situation. Feel free to take any of the surveys now, if you'd like. By the time you're done reading this book, you just might have some free videos waiting in your inbox!

SECTION ONE

MODEL

CHAPTER 2

Production—Every Leader's Greatest Responsibility

*Productivity is the engine that drives
your credibility and your leadership.*

—John Maxwell, *Good Leaders Ask Great Questions*

Your greatest responsibility as a leader is *not* to motivate others. It's to INSPIRE them! Think about this for a minute: What do you think inspired the Chicago Bulls to win six championships in eight years in the 1990s? Was it Michael Jordan's enthusiastic speeches before the games or his thirty points per game average? His "Game-Time WHOOO" chant before the game or his competitive drive that showed up every single play?

If you had to choose someone to lead your team, would you take the guy who averages over thirty points per game, was MVP (most valuable player) of the league five times, and has six rings, or the guy who is so passionate about the game that he screams and yells and gets everyone pumped up?

Don't get me wrong: when you have someone who does both, you have something very special. But if you study history, you'll learn many of these charismatic leaders have a tendency to make a lot of emotional errors, too. Brett Favre has the record for most interceptions thrown. Allen Iverson, Charles Barkley, and many other "charismatic" personalities never won a ring.

In the end, I'd rather follow someone who has a good record than someone who gives a good speech. The main reason I decided to join the John Maxwell Team at the age of twenty-nine was Maxwell's reputation for results, not his reputation for crowd engagement.

Coming from a long line of preachers, I actually am a very charismatic person, both on stage and off. I played in rock bands for years, and being on stage is one of the things I excel at the most. But at the age of twenty-five, I had just as much charisma, just as much creativity, and yet, no level of success to speak of because of my inability to produce.

I can still remember being in my early- and mid-twenties and finding myself so overwhelmed by my emotions and long-term vision that I would be lying in bed crying. I had such a huge passion for where I wanted to go in life, and yet no discipline to take any short-term steps toward making it happen. I could have gotten on stage and spoken to crowds. I could've inspired the masses. But no one wants to invite someone to speak who hasn't already *achieved* something.

Living Proof

The number-one mistake I see with up-and-coming leaders is that they want to share their message, but they don't want to **prove** their message. When I started my life-coaching business at the age of twenty-nine, I started hosting my own events to speak and promote my growth philosophies. The only people I could get in the door were my family and close friends. I had a professional video made, created a Facebook event that I invited everyone to, and managed to find sponsors for my event. But even the sponsors didn't bother to show up to hear me speak. Charity was the motivation for their support. The tax write-off was worth more to them than hearing what I had to say.

That very first time, I delivered one of my best ever presentations. I must've spent ten to fifteen hours preparing and rehearsing. I could quote that presentation in my sleep, and I did. I started having actual dreams about it! The problem was I had nothing to *prove* what I was saying. I didn't have any clients. I wasn't making any money. My business was basically nothing. So, why should people listen to me?

At the end of the presentation, I offered an eight-week, in-person mastermind program. The cost was around $200, and I made the most "killer offer" ever, as my mentor Paul Martinelli (President of the John Maxwell Team) had taught me. One of my friends owned a baking business and another, a local coffee shop. I provided free coffee and cookies for everyone as they arrived. And then for my closer, I offered a sign-on bonus of a pound of the coffee and two dozen of the cookies. Then to my surprise, my boss from my day job stood up and said, "If anyone buys Josh's package, I'll throw in a free gold-detail package on your vehicle, worth $200."

At this point, the sign-on bonuses basically made my mastermind group free. In fact, it was more like I was paying them to join! I'm still blown away by my own creativity putting something like this together on my very first sales attempt. To this day, I always offer some type of a killer offer on my virtual webinars, but I don't know that I've ever come close to that original offer!

Yet I didn't make one single sale. I got a whole lot of "That was great, man; I'm really proud of you" from everyone who was there. Unfortunately, pats on the back weren't going to pay my bills or make up for the money I had spent on all those cookies, coffee, and my new $99 suit from JCPenney.

Five years later: I've trained and mentored thousands of entrepreneurs and some of the top leaders in the network-marketing industry. Now, people fly me across the country to speak at their corporate events and to do workshops at their team retreats. Why? Because I put in the time to *prove my own message.*

When building my business in Tulsa, Oklahoma, seemed to get me nowhere, I took my business to social media. I began messaging everyone I knew who had any type of management or entrepreneurial position. Gradually, I realized that people in the network-marketing industry seemed to respond to me better. So then, I went all in, messaging anyone involved in network marketing. I started going through their friends list and friend-requesting other people from their companies.

Slowly but surely I began to pick up some clients. At one point, I decided to get crazy and make a goal to add ten clients per month. This goal instilled in me an even higher level of urgency to message everyone I could possibly find. I met those goals, and in my second year of business, was able to quit my full-time job detailing cars to become a full-time life coach. By that point, I was working with so many people that I had to launch virtual training groups that taught my life-coaching principles in more of a module format.

Here's what I found. The more successful I became, the more others were willing to take me at my word. If I said people should use Facebook Ads, they did. If I said people should use Instagram, they used it. If I said people should download every Grant Cardone audiobook that existed, they did. If I told people I used the "Self Journal" as my morning routine, they bought one. Motivating people became *easy* as I proved my own philosophies.

You First

A company of health and fitness coaches with which I've worked extensively has four vital behaviors for all their reps. Be a "product of the product" is one of those vital behaviors. The company encourages reps to make sure they're getting their *own results* with the products and programs they're selling.

Your results are the most important selling point you have, both as a salesperson and as a leader. If you're leading a team, they need to *see* you producing the thing you're asking them to do. If you're training people to sell, you need to be the top salesperson. If you're training people to recruit, be the top recruiter. Whatever message you're preaching, make sure you are also leading *by example*.

When I have my first one-on-one call with new clients, I always ask them to share their end-of-year goals with me. Then I ask them what is standing in their way. Almost every time, they tell me they don't have enough *performers* on their team. They say they need their team to step up, if they're going to hit their goals. The next thing I tell them is what I'm telling you now. *If you want your team to step up, you have to step up!* In every single, first-call with a client, I make that individual *up* his or her own production numbers. And yes, that's why I've coined the phrase #letspuketogether (I'll share more about this in a later chapter).

But shouldn't I be helping my team to hit bigger numbers? Absolutely. But how can you help others to improve if you aren't willing to do the same? Would you want to read this book if I were to tell you my sales have declined the last three years since I've started mentoring and "leading" others? Would you want to hear what I had to say if I were to mention that I've stopped selling so much, in order to raise up other leaders? You would think that was crazy. No one wants to learn from the person who is declining or stuck.

Your team is keenly aware of your level of ability and production. I promise you. If they feel your production has grown stagnant, that will act as their excuse to allow the same to happen in their business production. If they feel they have outgrown you, they won't follow you. Obviously, the end goal is for your team to surpass you and go on to lead their own teams. But your beginners and mid-level people should *never* outperform you. They should be chasing you!

Leaders who stop performing stop growing, stop learning, and have nothing new or relatable to teach. Isn't that the last kind of person you would want to follow? When you stop performing, you no longer have to learn. You don't know what new ways people are using to grow. You teach old systems that no longer work. While principles never change, sales and marketing is growing and evolving constantly. I would hate to learn from the leader who doesn't understand social media in this day and age.

Some of the companies I work with offer their reps free corporate mentors. These are people with college degrees (I'm assuming in business or sales), who give a company's top reps access to regular 1:1 calls for support and counsel in developing their leadership. Yet the top reps in these companies still are willing to pay me more money per hour than I used to make in a week of detailing cars for my support and counsel.

Now tell me why someone who has a *free* mentor would be willing to pay me that kind of money? Because unlike their corporate mentors, I've built my own online brand. I've learned how to market myself using social media, Facebook ads, email marketing, Instagram, and webinars. I've been on the phone making sales in a 1:1 setting. I've put in the *work to produce my own results*, something very few corporate mentors can say.

This is not to knock corporate mentors in any way. They usually understand things specific to their company like volume, rank advance, and bonus structures. They bring things to the table that an outsider would never understand the same way. But if you are one, please take the time to grow your own brand. Get on sales calls and learn what it takes. Put yourself in the trenches and learn what it means to look your biggest fears in the face. ***Producing is our greatest responsibility*** because it is the one thing that makes us continuously relatable. If you are not actually producing your own results, what can you possibly teach anyone other than pretty things you've read in a book? No one wants to hear what you've heard; they want to hear what you've *done!*

As I write this book, my mentor, John Maxwell, is seventy years old and still writing new books. He's still speaking at events. He's still helping businesses grow and still growing his own. He is the ideal modeler. The more he produces, the more inspired I am to see what I am capable of.

My mission statement says that I "PUSH entrepreneurs to live out their FULL potential." The greatest way to do this is to live out my ***own fullest potential*** first. Just as the greatest thing I can do for my children is to *show* them the way I want them to live.

Expanding Your Reach

How good of a leader am I If I don't have anyone to teach? Imagine that I have spent hundreds of hours (which I have) listening and learning from my mentor, John Maxwell, and now sit around helping ***no one*** with what I've gained! Leaders must have someone to lead. If I don't learn how to market myself, how to sell my programs, and how to *grow* my business, I may well be a good person, but I'm not a good leader.

How many good people do you know who aren't making a difference in the world at all? Are they, in any way, leaders? Does having good character in itself make you a good leader? What about if you have an abundance of insight to offer the world and never get off your own ass to offer it? I think it probably means the opposite. As Grant Cardone says, "The person who never steals anything, but also never gives anything, is the biggest crook of all."

I've known some amazing people with huge ambitions and tons of character who have never done anything to expand their reach. Give me people who are imperfect and rough around the edges, but willing to put themselves out there to help people *in spite* of their shortcomings. People spend thousands of dollars on courses to learn how to lead others properly, but they have no one to lead. They seek to become the perfect person—someone that people will randomly show up to serve and follow.

I grew up in a church where we spent *hours* praying for the "lost" to magically feel some tug on their hearts and, basically, show up at our church's front door and repent of their sins. We spent almost no time at all doing anything to go find, serve, and love these people. While we based our holiness on how much time we spent praying for people, in reality there were tons of "sinners" out there doing more for people than we were ever willing to do. I was in my twenties before I realized how many people in my church were in their fifties and sixties and still praying for people to find *them*. Thankfully, they also had taught me the principle of sowing and reaping, and I realized that, if they hadn't reaped any results after thirty years of sowing this particular seed, just maybe, there was a problem. At the age of twenty-six, I put together a rock band and hit the road to "preach" a message: Everyone has a dream worthy of chasing with action.

Can you imagine Steve Jobs creating the iPhone and then just sitting in his basement waiting for people to show up? Can you imagine a rock band spending $100K on producing the perfect song and then not spending just as much on advertising because they think the song should sell itself? Why are entrepreneurs so shortsighted sometimes?

Many people assume that the perfect strategy, the perfect wording, and the perfect skills (such as leadership) will manifest as alchemy, creating automatic sales and growth. But how can you possibly grow anything without other people? The whole point of leadership is to **help more people**. Which means that leadership can't even happen without recruiting people to lead *first*.

Once I heard a preacher say you should preach the Gospel everywhere you go—and use words when necessary. The point? Christians can be the biggest hypocrites in the world because we are so quick to speak and so slow to act. I, myself, am a Christian, though I've grown up in a world that has made me think twice about even calling myself a Christian. Modern-day Christianity looks very little like the faith that Jesus preached. Jesus touched the untouchable. He forgave the unforgivable. Jesus was the ultimate example—*acting bigger than he spoke*. He said some pretty incredible things. But his *actions* spoke so much louder.

My challenge to you is to act bigger than you speak. My challenge is to completely undo your ideas of what it means to be a leader, and then, to rebuild from the ground up. Grow your conviction of **being** that someone, not just looking or sounding like someone who fits a glittering image of a leader.

As John Maxwell has said so many times, we should seek to grow more on the inside than we do on the outside. In this book, I'm going to teach you to **grow** into the person that everyone *wants* to follow. Not because you're louder than everyone else, but because you've earned their trust and have credibility. PS: You'll also be louder than everyone because action *always* makes noise and draws attention.

If producing results is your biggest problem, I've got some more tips for you in the next chapter. But I want you to pause for two minutes and take this simple survey that will help you pinpoint your struggle. If you go to **joshcoats.com/survey**, you'll find a simple questionnaire that you can take. This survey was designed around the top struggles that I find people facing. My team will send you the results of your survey along with a free resource that will help you address your specific situation. While I'd like to think that this book will help everyone, I want to send you something personal that will address your specific struggle.

CHAPTER 3
PUKE Goals (Urgency)

Productivity must become a high priority on your list of things to do as a leader. But how can that happen without setting new goals? A lot of leaders are excellent at challenging others to set new goals, yet never manage to do so themselves. An essential part of becoming a top producer is being someone who continually sets new goals.

Someone who is always reaching for something new is someone who is always forced to grow. So, I want to teach you my philosophy around goal setting. Of the different things I teach, I believe this is probably the *most valuable thing I've created for my clients*. Like them, you're about to hate my guts for a short period of time.

And then it will blow your business out of the water, and you'll decide to love me again. Or as I like to say, "Six days a week you hate me, one day a week you love me!" Payday might be the only day you really appreciate what I'm about to teach you. This is what caused me to coin the phrase #letspuketogether!!! Because once you learn my goal-setting strategies, you'll want to puke!

Why are some people growing and others continuing to fail? Early in 2017, I sat down and asked myself that question. I had helped two different people go Top Ten in their network-marketing business—an award that is given out annually in their company based on sales and leadership, where the numbers start over every year. In

2016, I had helped seven or eight of my 1:1 clients go Elite for the first time, something that puts them in the top .02% of production for their company.

Another person used my $200 training, The Art of Recruiting, to take her business to a new level and then go Top Ten two years in a row. I watched countless others go through my groups and see incredible results. And yet, I also watched ten times that number of people go through my groups and say things like, "I didn't see any measurable results, but I feel so much more confident!" That's my least favorite thing in the world to hear!

I decided to take a higher level of responsibility for people paying me money. I wanted people to see **measurable results** if they were going to give me money. Over time, I realized that 80 percent of these people came to me looking for someone to "fix" them. They thought that because I had helped someone they looked up to, I had some type of magic wand I could wave and trick people into working harder. They thought that having "access" to me would somehow magically turn them into production unicorns. But those people never grew. THE ONLY PEOPLE WHO REALLY GREW WERE THE ONES WHO CAME TO ME WITH SPECIFIC AND URGENT GOALS.

Remember the people I mentioned who I helped go Elite and Top Ten? Many of those people came to me and said something like this: "Josh, I have this crazy goal that I want to hit and I don't even know if it's possible. I'm afraid to even say it out loud. Can you help?" YES! Not only can I help, but this is what I LIVE for! (If you have crazy, massive goals, you'd better contact me!) I took each one of them on with confidence, not even knowing whether the goal was possible. But believing that anyone who wants something badly enough can make it happen with the right focus and intentionality, I said yes anyway.

The people who didn't grow, who didn't get what they paid for, are the people who showed up with nothing to fight for. They said they wanted it to work. They said they wanted to grow. But they really didn't have any true *urgency* to make it happen.

Now, I'm going to teach you how to create URGENCY in your business. If you apply it, this will change your life forever. If you teach it, it will change your teams' lives forever. Urgency is the thing I teach in all my trainings and with all my clients. On Instagram, it has created a revolution of people using my hash tag #letspuketogether. When I first started teaching this, people started to say things like, "Oh my God, I think I'm going to vomit." My response was, "Then let's puke together, baby!"

What Do You REALLY Want?

It's all about creating urgency. First, ask yourself: "What do I REALLY want?" Or as I ask my 1:1 clients on our first call together: "If I could remove all obstacles, take away all pain, time, money, and limits, and you could just reach out and grab ANYTHING you want, what would it be?" All of a sudden, they're able to think clearly. They're finally able to see what they really want, instead of what they think is possible. And yet most people *still* can't carry it through.

Watching them on our zoom call, I see their eyes light up as they *start* to think about what they really want. But then, even as their head, confidence, and stature is rising, I see it happen. Almost every time. As if in slow motion, they run right into their limiting beliefs on their way up to reaching for what they really want.

Just as their eyes begin to see the impossible, it's like a demon perches on their left shoulder and shows them their limitations and their perceived reality, and then, in one fell swoop, they come crashing right back down to reality. Their entire posture changes. Now looking downward, they slouch their shoulders and their energy level sinks into defeat. They stammer something like, "Well, I only have this many people that really want to grow, so I think I could probably ..."

"NOOOOOOOOO!" I interrupt. "I don't want you to think about what you currently have. I don't want you to think about what's realistic or attainable. I just want you to think about what you *really want*. When we ask the next question, we'll figure out *how* to get it."

You see, if you always base your goals on what you currently have, you'll never be forced to get creative about how to get something new. Steve Jobs didn't sit down with a flip phone and ask, "How could I make this better?" That's what everyone else did. And so, cell phones evolved ever so slowly for so long. Each year, one millimeter slimmer, one extra snake game. Between 2000 and 2006, the only thing they figured out how to do was make the phone fold in half and turn a music clip into a ringtone so you could annoy every person in the room with your favorite song every time someone called.

Steve Jobs sat down and asked, "WHAT DO I WANT?" And he realized he didn't even want a phone. He wanted a music-playing, web-surfing device that would fit into your pocket and could also make phone calls, if needed. Everyone else was trying to figure out how to make a better phone. Jobs was asking how to revolutionize culture. He couldn't do that with the current pieces available, so he hired people who could invent the technology he saw in his imagination.

Base your goals on what you currently have and you may find a way to improve your business, but you'll never revolutionize it.

You'll find yourself creating something that is 2 percent better than what you've done. Hardly worth waking up early for. Once you realize what you *really* want, that very desire will create **three things that will absolutely change your life**:

- Focus
- Creativity
- Ownership

Urgency Creates Focus

I can still remember going into my second year in business. I'd just spent an entire year turning my wheels. Going to networking groups, cold-calling, taking people out for coffee, and even putting on my own events (if that's what you could call it when eight of your family members and two coworkers show up). In addition, I was trying every trick that podcasts were teaching me. Trying to create a website, a podcast, a YouTube channel, while also posting on Facebook and Instagram … it was exhausting. But most of all, it was unprofitable.

I always joke with my training groups that it's one thing to be exhausted with a fat paycheck, but quite another when you don't even have a check to show for it. At the beginning of my second year, I sat down with a big calendar and decided to set my own "puke" goal (I didn't have that terminology yet, of course). I wrote a big "10" at the top right corner of the first page. And then, I decided what I'd need to accomplish each week to make that happen. I wrote a big "3" at the end of each week. I figured it was better to go past my goal instead of coming up short.

Let me just tell you that in my whole first year of business, I'd signed two clients and made about $500. To be clear, I'd signed *two clients* in my whole first year, and now here I was writing down a goal to sign ten *that month*. I was going to try to pull off three clients—more than I'd managed during my first year—each week!?

Here's the thing: It scared me. But I was sick of playing small-time. I was sick of not getting the kind of results I really wanted. And I was sick of making excuses. So as hard as it was, as crazy as it seemed, I wrote down the numbers anyway.

Here's what happened: I was forced to **immediately** put together a more *focused* plan. There's no way in the world I could possibly do the thirty-two things on my to-do list and still talk to enough people to make that many sales. So I decided that from now on, if it didn't put money in my pocket, I wasn't doing it! And really, the **only** thing that put money in my pocket was talking to people.

What soon became apparent was that I could talk to more people on social media in an hour than I could in a week in-person, without leaving my house, without wasting gas money and driving time. So, I redirected my time and energy into posting and messaging people on social media. Posting only took five to ten minutes, so I spent the rest of my time messaging people and offering them my services. Other than that, I would continue doing my own Personal Development to make sure I kept myself growing and modeling the thing I was selling.

That was it! Game plan was so simple it almost sounds ridiculous! But guess what? That amped-up level of urgency forced me into such an intense focus that I found myself signing ten clients that month, and actually spending *less* time working my business. I repeated this process all year long and, by October, I was making enough money to comfortably walk away from my full-time job. I ended up making $48K that second year working part-time. Quite the improvement from year one I'd say.

One of the first things people tell me when I help them set a "puke goal" (as I call them) is something along these lines: "But Josh, I don't want one of those businesses where I work all day and night and never have time for my family." You see, my reputation precedes me. And based on the kind of results I've helped people achieve, they assume my strategy looks something like this: Work more, sleep less, become a zombie who hates life. But that is *not* what getting results has to look like. They're stuck in an "or" mentality. They think you can be more successful *or* have time freedom. But why would anyone settle for OR when AND is always an option.

When you are committed to a goal that looks and feels impossible, for the very first time in your business, you are forced to *focus* like never before. Instead of working more hours, you simply find a way to finally do the *right* things within the hours that you do choose to work. Instead of checking your notifications, you make a to do list.

In my training groups, I make everyone work from a daily tracker that forces them to get the right things done every day. As a result, I have people telling me they're working harder than they've ever worked before, and yet they feel like they have more family time. More importantly, they feel like they have more attention to give their families because they're not thinking all night about what they have or haven't completed in their business. They're done. They did the right things, and now, they can go about their day with confidence, knowing they're moving in the right direction.

This is what I want for you, too. I want you make *more* money than you've ever made, helping more people than you've ever helped, spending *less* time thinking and worrying about your business. Urgency forces focus, and focus always produces more results in less time.

Start by setting a puke goal for the year. Ask yourself what you would accomplish if nothing stood in your way. Then ask yourself what kind of monthly and weekly numbers it would take to make that happen. You can't know for sure, but what kind of numbers would make you feel confident about hitting a goal that big? Now write a simple list of daily tasks you'll have to do to make those things happen.

Steve Jobs didn't have a perfect product with his first iPhone. But what he had was something that was so much closer to the thing he was envisioning. It's not a failure to have something less than you imagined. Everything is a work in progress. It's only a failure if you don't try to imagine something better. That's a good way to end up being a flip phone in the age of smartphones.

Urgency Breeds Creativity

In year three of my business, knowing that messaging people had got me to where I was, I needed a new and crazier puke goal to do something even bigger. I had noticed that Lewis Howes's Facebook ads were showing up in my news feed *all* the time! In fact, sometimes Facebook would refresh the feed, and one Lewis Howes ad would disappear only for another one to appear. What was this guy doing?

I didn't know anything about ads. But I was smart enough to know that if everyone else was seeing his ads as often as I was, this guy must be killing it. And after reading *The 10X Rule* by Grant Cardone and deciding to try to "10X" the previous year's income, I was diligently searching for ways to make it happen. I had made about $40K per year detailing cars, so I decided to "puke" and add a zero to that for my new annual goal. $400K was about what I had made during the previous ten years of my life. Knowing how crazy this was, I made a secondary goal to take over everyone's news feeds the same way Lewis had taken over mine. I had no idea how to do it, but I was going to figure it out!

When you have an urgent goal, you first find a new focus. And if that level of urgency is not enough for you to hit your goal, you uncover your creativity! I believe that every single one of us is born with infinite creativity; we just do not always feel impelled to use it. And the beauty of urgency is that it drives you to tap into that place deep inside.

A month later, I was on a call with one of my clients, and she mentioned having a Facebook Ads course she'd paid for that she hadn't done anything with. I offered to give her the next call for free if she'd give me access to the training. She was more than happy to make the trade. For the next three months, I would sit in my office at the end of my day watching those modules. I forced myself to try everything I was told to try. I forced myself to experiment, to fail, to just keep trying until it made sense. It seemed like rocket science for the first two months. But then, it started to click. It started to become second nature.

Halfway into the year, one of my clients gave me an idea. By then, I had created a business model out of signing a 1:1 client, and then offering to speak for their team for free to advertise my training. Every time I signed a new client, usually a company leader, I was able to speak to their team, resulting in my getting tons of new followers and some new customers in my training groups. It was a great model but was starting to fill my schedule with evening calls that took time away from my family.

My client's company was having an annual event they called Summit; around 20,000 people would be attending. But year after year, people would leave this event and go home unchanged. Lots of excitement would be generated, but that pretty much wore off after a week and nothing came of the Summit in terms of improving their business. He suggested I do one big call that *everyone* would be invited to. I would teach their attendees how to keep up the momentum long after coming home from their annual event.

Up until this time, the only way someone got access to me as a public speaker was the one time I spoke for their own team's call. I'd held twenty or thirty team calls over the last several months, and according to my client, there were tons of people who would be excited to get that access again. So, I took his advice and I created a Facebook event, sending out invites to all my clients. Six weeks later, we had 4,200 people who RSVP'd for the event.

When I went live on Facebook for the event, we got up to 1,200 people live … and then it crashed. Facebook couldn't handle the amount of comments that were coming through during the live stream. Everyone was so excited that the *comments* and *likes* were going crazy. Some people were commenting and saying, "STOP COMMENTING EVERYONE; it's causing the stream to lag out!" But the excitement was too much. It crashed. We broke the internet!

I tried again. Thought maybe it was just a bad connection. Once again, we got up to 1,200 people, and once again, the hordes of likes and comments crashed it. Here I was, with potentially 4,200 people waiting to hear me speak, thousands (if not tens of thousands) of dollars in potential sales just waiting for me!

Eventually, I decided to open a Google Hangout. I spent thirty minutes on the phone talking back and forth with two of my clients who tried to help me figure out how to use Google Hangout. Finally, I had a line open, and even after all of that, 840 people stuck with me to hear my presentation. The video on YouTube ended up getting over 6000 views as others shared it. That was the biggest weekend I'd ever had! I made as much that *month* as I had the entire previous year, not to mention a whole new way of doing business.

My new strategy for 10X-ing my business fell into place: I would integrate Facebook ads with webinars that I would use to expand my network and close sales—*all in one night*. To this day, I use this strategy, and it continues to bring in new people month after month! The point of this story is not to convince you to do Facebook ads or webinars, but to teach you the *power of urgency mixed with creativity*.

Because my goal was so crazy, I forced myself to think outside the box. I forced myself to be always *seeking* new opportunities. My ears, my mind, and my heart were wide open to receive. One of the universal principles I believe in more than anything else in life is that whatever you seek, you will *find*. If you want drama, you'll find it! If you want an excuse, there will be plenty to choose from. But it's just as easy to find peace and solutions when they are what you are consciously looking for.

How many trainings have you done where you heard something that blew your mind, and yet you just never implemented it? How many new systems have you learned that you tried for only three to six weeks before deciding they didn't work? The one year that my business struggled was in 2017. That particular year, I lost my urgency. I got comfortable. I was consistently making more in a month than I had previously made in a year, and I let myself just get comfortable.

I stopped getting creative. I stopped evolving. And as a result, I almost lost it all. When I finally pulled my head out of my ass, I got right back to the basics—what I had just spent three years teaching. I started setting monthly puke goals. I hustled. I got creative. And as I'm writing this book, I am about to have my record month.

I learned my lesson the hard way. And I made myself a promise to never lose that creativity again. Now I'm creating more streams using free resources that bring people into my funnel, writing more material, and working with a marketing team that's raised my Facebook ads to another level. I've launched a podcast (Your PUSH Coach) and even have my own app (also Your PUSH Coach).

I'm not saying anyone needs to have all of those things. But the second I got my momentum back, I swore I'd do whatever it takes to make sure I'm always moving forward and never standing still again. When you have the proper momentum on your side, you can start to create ideas that you pay others to implement. It sounds like I'm doing a million things. In reality, the power of *focus* that I taught you has me doing the things I enjoy the most, while others are putting my ideas into action for me.

Urgency Demands Ownership

When I signed up for the John Maxwell Team, my first assignment was to read his book, *The 21 Irrefutable Laws of Leadership*, three times. Honestly, I was a little pissed. I just paid my entire tax return as the down payment, and you're going to tell me to go read a book … three times … before I can access anything that I've actually paid for? I had never actually read a total of three books in my entire life.

I can remember reading *The Outsiders* (sooooo good) and *The Indian in the Cupboard*. I was one of those smart-but-lazy kids—smart enough to get really good grades without trying all that hard because I was an outstanding test taker. I could memorize anything and BS my way through anything, including book reports. Except for that one time I was supposed to read *Huckleberry Finn* but instead watched the movie *Tom and Huck*. I didn't know they were different stories. I failed the test, and my English teacher knew exactly why!

"Josh," he said, as he waved me to come up to the desk. "Did you watch the movie?"

"Of course not!" I lied through my teeth.

"Are you sure? Because by the sounds of these answers, I think you may have watched the wrong movie. These answers make sense if you watched *Tom and Huck*, but you were supposed to read *Huckleberry Finn*."

Busted!

Naturally, I fell in love with personal development through listening to podcasts and audiobooks, *not* reading actual books. So, this was going to be a stretch. Nonetheless, I was committed to the journey. So, I got the book and sat down to read. Chapter one, page one, paragraph one changed my life. One sentence alone was worth more than the value of what I had paid to go through the training.

I'm not even going to quote the book. Instead, I'm going to tell you what I remember, because this is what stuck: "You'll never be more successful than your ability to help people." This is one of those instances when what you hear is more valuable than what was said. Because J Max was teaching a leadership principle. The point was that your team will never grow beyond your leadership skills. So, your success depends on how much work you put into learning to lead others. But I saw it as an ***ownership law***.

As I read this one sentence, my whole life flashed before me like someone in a movie who is about to die. I thought back to the small churches I grew up volunteering in. I heard pastor after pastor saying things like, "You know, this church could double in size if everyone would invite just one person." Meanwhile, the pastor himself never once brought a guest. I heard them saying things like, "This church could do more good if more people would volunteer" or "if more people would give" or "if people would show up on time" or "if people were as serious about their faith as I am."

I thought back to local guitar shops where I used to hang out on my days off. The owners would say things like, "Local shops don't stand a chance when Guitar Center is building massive stores and has more buying power. Their prices are too cheap to compete against because of their buying power." Or "Guitar Center stays open later than we can afford to" or "Guitar Center lets punk kids sit around shredding on guitars turned up too loud."

Local coffee-shop owners were saying, "People don't even value real coffee anymore; they just want dessert drinks from Starbucks" or "They have a drive-thru" or "We can't afford to be open seven days a week."

In that moment, I saw the truth of it: Every struggling person I'd ever been around, or who I'd spent most of my life respecting, had always blamed their own problems on everyone else. I have never heard a pastor say, "I'm going to learn marketing so we can grow" or "Maybe if I brought guests I could change the culture" or "Maybe if I learned to teach people about things *they* valued, I could help them to see what I see."

I never heard the guitar store say, "If Guitar Center is open until 8:00 p.m., let's stay open until 9:00 p.m." or "Maybe we should give our customers a better experience" or "I guess being closed on Sunday and Monday just isn't an option anymore, so maybe we should hire another person."

I made God and myself a promise that day that I would NEVER blame my lack of success on anything or anyone else. That day, I realized that I, alone, am responsible for either my success or my failure. But either way, it's on me. This is one of the main reasons I was able to stick with my business through the hard times in year one, when I wasn't seeing any results, and in year four, when I got lazy. Instead of blaming it on others, instead of finding an excuse, I forced myself to keep seeking solutions. I would look in the mirror, over and over, and remind myself, "You have no one else to blame."

Now let me take a second to explain what ownership is and what it isn't. Ownership is taking the credit even when things are going bad. What ownership is *not* is using a lack of results as any way of measuring your self-worth or value as a human.

Ownership is simply a means of grading, a scale of your performance. If your kid tries out for a team and doesn't make it, that doesn't mean he or she is not worthy of being on the team. It just means that he/she has more work to do. Maybe the others started playing at a younger age. Maybe the other players have more natural talent. Either way, you tell your kid to keep practicing. You may hire a private coach or mentor to help out. Maybe a specialized summer camp to get extra training. But it does *not* mean your kid is less than the other kids. It just means your kid's *skill* has not caught up to the others. Ownership is realizing you have the power to do and become anything you want. And if you haven't arrived there *yet*, it just means there's more work to do.

When you fully understand this concept of ownership, you will realize I've just handed you the greatest blessing and curse you've ever received. The greatest curse because you'll never have a reason to blame anyone else for the struggles you endure. The greatest blessing because you'll realize that, if no one else has the power to give or deny your success, then no one else has the ability to hold you back from success. Not an unsupportive spouse, not the Instagram algorithm, not a bad upline. NOTHING!

Own Your Mission

Pretend, for a minute, that you have left the house for the night, your kids (or pets) remaining home with a babysitter. You've been out all night having drinks and enjoying yourself, (or maybe just at Target trying everything on!). On your way home, you realize there's smoke coming from your neighborhood. Strange. You get to your neighborhood and realize the smoke is coming from your street. As you round the corner onto your street, it is clear that the smoke is coming from your house! Your house is up in flames. You race your car up the street. You have no idea whether or not your loved ones are okay. You drive up into the front yard, not caring that you just demolished your lawn and shrubs, and run to the door.

Somewhere in between the car and the house, you lose your keys. You're in such a frantic state that you have no idea what happened. Maybe they fell out in the car, maybe they're buried in the bottom of your purse. All you know is that the front door is locked, your loved ones are probably inside, and you have no keys. What do you do? Do you kick down the door? Punch through a window? Run through the wall? Yes, Yes, and HELL, YES! You *find* a way to get in because you have no other choice.

Now, lost keys. Let's take away the fire and take away your loved ones being home. Do you still kick down the door and ruin your new Jimmy Choo shoes? Or do you go sit in your car, call a locksmith, and play on your phone until someone shows up to get you in? My guess is the latter.

Here's the thing. I've spent hundreds, if not thousands, of hours on calls with people just like you. I've listened to story after story on 1:1 calls, in my training groups, and at the team retreats I've done around the country. I've heard people tell me how desperate they are for this business to work for them. I've heard stories of people with jobs that are eating their souls and keeping them away from making memories with their kids. Stories of stay-at-home moms who want nothing more than to relieve the financial pressures on a spouse who is overworked and underpaid. (He wants to be a good dad to your kids but doesn't even have the energy to show love, to them or you, after working so hard all day.) Stories of people buried in debt so deep, they feel no hope of ever having any type of financial freedom. People who want to travel, send their kids to the best schools, give to charity, raise funds for others in need.

From what I've seen, there are a whole lot of houses on fire, and a bunch of #momboss's sitting around in their cars, playing on their phones, waiting for a locksmith to come save the day. "But I don't have enough followers" or "I don't know how to talk to people" or "Why would anyone want to sign up with me?" just sounds to me like, "I don't care enough about my family to run into the burning building."

The truth is that you have the same scripts, same tools, same resources as everyone else. You're just looking for something easier. My best-selling training to date is called the Art of Recruiting. It's so full of content you can't possibly walk away and NOT know how to sell and recruit. People tell me all the time how much they loved the training. How inspiring and impactful it was. In reality, only 10 to 15 percent of the people who have taken the training actually did anything with it.

How do I know? Because the views on the week-four videos are less than half of the views on week one. Because by week three, hardly anyone is even checking into the Facebook group we provide. And because the people who do the work, that 10 to 15 percent, end up having crazy-positive testimonials.

So, I decided to change the game. In 2018 I launched a training called the PUSH Mastermind. In this group, I give people the same daily-activities list, but instead of giving them twenty videos to view, we have a once-a-week teaching call. Instead of trying to teach people *how* to build their businesses, I put the focus on just *doing* the work.

Daily challenges, weekly call-outs for falling behind on activities, and weekly recognition for people getting results—all the same principles I'll teach you in the mentoring section. Now that the way I'm training people has completely changed, instead of hearing things like, "O-MY-Gaaaaaawd, you dropped so many truth bombs, Josh!" (I'm saying this in my best "diva" voice), I hear things like, "I've never worked this hard at any time in my entire business. And it feels GOOD to be this productive!" Instead of having 10 to 15 percent of the enrollees sticking it out, we have over 90 percent. The testimonials are piling up. Now I have a very simple Five Day Recruiting Challenge people can go through if they do need to brush up on their recruiting skills. You can get in and get out and then get right back to work.

I get that my "house on fire" analogy is a little extreme, but that's how serious I am about helping people to create their best lives. I'm continually reminding my PUSH groups that the demons you don't face are the ones you automatically pass on to your kids. Like for real, this is serious business! You can tell your kids all day and night to chase their dreams. But if you don't **show** them what that looks like, will they? I can promise you they'll duplicate what you **do**, not what you say.

Do you really want to tell your kids that they're not "outgoing enough, pretty enough, or skilled enough" to make their dreams come true? Do you want to teach them that working a job that eats your soul alive is the norm? Or that not having enough money to go on vacations is the norm? Or to be swimming in debt? Because if you don't put in the work it takes to change your own situation, your kids will grow up with these same limiting beliefs.

You'll have to pray they find a PUSH Coach willing to help them move forward because you weren't willing to do it by setting the right example. To me, that's the only way to fail as a parent. To just never love them enough to try to change their stars. Perfection is something that is far from attainable. But you better believe I will fight with everything I have to give my kids the best that I can.

Ownership isn't just about you. It's also about what you're willing to do for your family, and for the world around you. Even if your house isn't on fire. Even if you have plenty of money in the bank, have a boat, a white picket fence. Do you have enough to fund your favorite charity? Do you have enough to build orphanages in Africa? Do you have enough to end world hunger? If not, you're not done yet.

Grant Cardone says, "Success is your moral and ethical obligation." And I believe in that statement so much. When my business struggled in year four, I could no longer afford to write the check for others. I didn't have the energy to think about the world around me that I wanted to help. But if you're house isn't on fire, I believe very strongly that *your mission* should be to help as many other people as possible to put their fires out. As long as you are breathing, there is work to do—because there are others who need you! Living anything less than your FULL potential is a slap in the face to both your creator and the rest of creation.

CHAPTER 4
Leaders Are Listeners

I've heard person after person say they're convinced they can't be good leaders because they're not outgoing enough. They don't "talk good." While I do believe you need to have some solid people skills to be able to lead, what you don't need is to be that person who does all of the talking. As a leader, I've helped a lot more people when I was listening than when I was talking.

This concept is twofold. First, let's talk about helping individuals through listening, and then, I'll help you learn how to help the masses through listening.

When I first signed up for the John Maxwell Team, I felt pretty confident I'd be a good speaker. I come from a long line of preachers, and if there's one gift every male in my family (and my cousin, Robin) had, it was the gift of gab. We could talk your ear off. A Coats family Christmas at my grandpa's consisted of everyone in the room competing for "loudest in the room" to try to work a joke in. My grandpa and two uncles were known for reading and memorizing joke books that they would use as icebreakers in their sermons. If you've ever thought of church as a boring thing, it's because you never sat through one of my grandpa's services. He could make you laugh, cry, celebrate, and repent, all in thirty minutes.

One of the greatest honors I've ever received was my certification in life coaching. But early in my training, I kept hearing this word being used over and over in the curriculum, and it really scared me: listening. Christian Simpson, one of the smartest people you'll ever meet, created the curriculum on life coaching for the John Maxwell Team. He beat this one thing into our brains: True coaching is listening, not talking. Now that sounded like something I would just be absolutely terrible at. But as I listened to the purpose behind this brief message, my mind was absolutely blown.

The way he explained it is that traditional coaching is screaming and yelling at other people, and really more of a motivational and mentoring role. But *true coaching* is when you ask people questions to help them to find their own answers. And then, you listen to what they have to say. You help them find their own truth. This immediately grabbed my attention. While the thought of listening for a living scared me, the idea of *helping people find their own answers*, with no strings attached, gave me a new life purpose.

I grew up in a very traditional Christian home. In the churches we attended, we were taught that you were either with us or against us. You were either on our side or on the wrong side. In my early twenties, I worked with a mentor who taught me the greatest lesson I've ever learned—the importance of continual growth—but who also constantly questioned my ability to do that on my own. When I decided I wanted to do music instead of ministry, I was told I wasn't thinking clearly and that my gifts for preaching were too good to ignore. He told me time and time again that his plan was better than mine. And as a result, I began to resent him.

The crazy thing is that he was right. I really did end up being a preacher, in the sense that I now have a career talking, not playing music. But by constantly trying to force me down a path I didn't want, he lost the right to help me find my path. And the reality is that music did eventually lead me to this path. By simply taking the step I had in front of me, it led me to saying yes to the next opportunity: the John Maxwell Team. Had I listened to that mentor, I may have never even found the John Maxwell Team.

I had already decided I would never do that to another person for as long as I live (at least not intentionally). I would support people regardless of whether I agreed with their decisions. I would help people find their own paths, not follow mine. When my good friend, Ben, told me that he was moving to Texas and leaving my band without a drummer, right in the middle of our tour promoting our latest album we had worked so hard on, I happily gave him my blessing.

(Can I just tell you something? No one needs your blessing to do what they want. So, why don't you just go ahead and give it to them if it will help them to follow their path with more peace and confidence?)

Therefore, when Christian Simpson told me I could make a career out of doing exactly that, helping people find their path and then giving them permission and support in walking down that path, I knew I had to do whatever it took to learn this practice.

Respect Breeds Respect

I'm going to teach you a few things about this practice so that you can use this same approach to help your team. As a leader, if you aren't careful, if you find yourself trying to strong-arm people into following your path, you'll only end up murdering any influence you may have with them. On the other hand, if you properly coach them, not only will you find that, 90 percent of the time, they end up finding the path you were going to point them down anyways, but also that they trust and respect you more than ever. Why? For no other reason than this: You respected them and gave them the freedom to find it themselves.

Zig Ziglar says that if you don't give people a door out, they'll look for one. Essentially, effective coaching gives people the freedom to find any door they want, which engenders in them complete trust in the coach to walk them through the process.

So, here's the secret. This is how you properly coach people to find their own path:

- ◆ You simply ask them questions instead of giving them answers.
- ◆ You take the time and be curious enough to listen to them, instead of trying to take charge of them.

Instead of saying, "You really need to do this," you take the time to ask, "What do you think you should do about this?" And then, you listen to the answer. Sometimes my clients try to ask me questions about what's working for everyone else. Sometimes I'm human and I tell them. But when I'm doing my job properly, I stop them and ask them to forget what everyone else is doing and think instead about what success would look like for them.

Start with the End

My favorite coaching tactic in the world is to simply remind people to start with the end in mind. I'm sure you've heard this quote used many times in many ways, but for me it is my philosophy on everything I do. I'm constantly challenging my clients who feel stuck about their next step to ask, instead, what the desired end result looks like. Because if you can just get yourself to imagine where you want to eventually end up, deciding what's next is almost always clear. You do the thing that gets you closer to said end result.

Sometimes that's similar to what others are doing and sometimes it looks nothing like what others are doing.

I had to have one of these moments with myself. I've worked really hard on my Instagram account lately, growing it to almost twenty thousand, but honestly, not really seeing measurable results. I had to ask myself, what is the end result? Is Instagram really getting me closer to my end result, or am I spending a bunch of time there because everyone else is? Do I really want to spend my time where everyone else is? Or do I want to spend my time where I make the most money?

For me personally, Facebook ads allow me to be in any feed I choose by spending money, not time. And for me the end goal is *always* to get more results with less time. Anytime I can use money to buy time, I'm in—100 percent. If Instagram works for you, keep doing it! If not, ask yourself how much time it should be getting.

This isn't a conversation about Instagram or Facebook; this is simply a question of what do you want? This key question is something you have to constantly ask yourself, not to mention, the people you are mentoring. What do YOU want? Not what do I want for you. As Christian said so many times, "It is arrogant and ignorant to assume someone else can get the same results by doing the same thing." Let that sink in for a minute!

If your game plan is to get everyone to copy you, then you're assuming every person has the same strengths, talents, and resources that you do. That doesn't mean that I'm against teaching systems. I'm a *firm* believer in duplicatable systems. But I also believe that systems are for teaching the masses. There's really no point in working with people individually if all you're going to do is repeat the same system you already taught on a team training.

When people are using the system and still struggling, they need personalized help in the form of coaching. Otherwise, I would have one system on my website that I would call THE MASTER SYSTEM. And it would cost $10,000, and I would sleep in until noon every day. But my systems are for the masses, to give people some type of process to implement and a strategy to move forward. My one-on-one time, on the other hand, is reserved for coaching people. Which means I'm helping them find *their own voice* within the system. Their own personalized ways of working the system that will leverage their singular strengths and be in alignment with their goals.

So, when you are speaking to the masses, please create systems, standard operating procedures, and duplicatable systems. But when you are seeing someone who has earned personal time (I'll talk more about qualifying people in another chapter), please take the time to listen. Get curious about what's going on in his or her business. Assume nothing. The only safe assumption to make is that the problem is unique and that the same answer you gave last time is not the same answer this person needs.

The Real Story

Remember this: The first answer someone gives you is never the real problem—it is just the story. One of the only quotes I've coined myself says: *Our limiting beliefs are constantly looking for a story to justify our fears and excuses.* Meaning, we all tend to make up a story to explain why we are struggling that sounds much better than the real problem. If you're sleeping in every day and rushing into your day, you'll say something like, "I'm feeling overwhelmed. I'm so busy working my business that I don't have time for my family. I think I need to take a step back from my business."

The real problem? You are sleeping in, getting your business started too late, and then not completing your business tasks before your family gets home. Because you know you need to finish your tasks, you're working on your phone with one hand, while trying to cook dinner with the other. Because of this, you can't think straight. Your kid is just asking you something simple like what you're fixing for dinner. But because your brain is trying to focus on two things at a time, you have no room for a question from your kid, and you end up yelling. Your problem is NOT that this business is taking time away from your family. Your problem is you're sleeping in.

And yet the typical advice a coach would give in this situation, if no probing questions were asked, is that this person needs to plan out the day better—make sure to use a to-do list and stick to it. While that is a great answer, it wouldn't address the main issue because not enough questions were posed to find out this individual's specific circumstances.

If you get curious enough, and ask enough questions, the real problem will come out. But if you just try to solve the problem immediately, without engaging the person in a questioning process, all you'll be trying to solve is the story, not the root of the problem. That person will never be able to move forward because that hidden root will still be there, anchoring him/her in place.

Global Listening

Now, here's where this gets really fun. Remember that I mentioned I would help you to use questions to help the masses? The most beautiful thing is when you get good enough at asking questions that you start to accumulate data. J Max calls this *global listening*. Global listening is when you're listening with curiosity so that you can help the individual you're talking to. But you're also smart enough to realize that, if this one individual has this problem and has created this story, there's a good chance many other people have the same problems, and often, the same stories.

When my business for life coaching first started taking off, my schedule rapidly filled, and I had a new problem. My business was making money, but not enough to quit my job. Yet, as long as I was working my job, I didn't have enough hours in the day to take on more clients. I was stuck trying to balance a full-time job and a part-time business, not knowing how to keep growing.

And then one day, I grabbed coffee with Scott Taylor. I had gone through a list of local business owners, messaging all of them to see if they wanted to grab coffee. The goal was twofold: network with other business people and look for an opening to life coach them and earn their business. I was usually pretty good at getting the convo going and asking questions that would lead to the other person opening up about their struggles ... then BOOM! ... I would work my life-coaching skills to help them find a solution.

Well, this meeting didn't exactly go my way (and yet it did!). When we sat down for coffee, Scott took immediate control by asking me questions. Most people falsely believe that the person who is talking is leading the convo, but any negotiator can tell you the same thing my mentor, Randy Stroman, once taught me: The one who asks the questions controls the negotiation. This is because the person asking is the one who learns the most valuable information. The questioner then can use what was learned against the other person in the case of negotiating, or *for* the person when it comes to coaching. I began to explain to him my struggles: I was always running out of time to get everything done but needed more growth in my business before I could quit my job. Scott said, "It sounds to me like you are trading your time for money. You need to find some way of selling to the masses. You need to write a book or a curriculum or something."

Fueled by twenty ounces of cold brew and stuck in rush-hour traffic, my brain began to work. I started thinking about how many times on a 1:1 call I had heard the exact same problems, and how my questions led people to coming up with the same solutions. Framing this scenario in light of a way to provide value to the masses gave me the ability to make use of what I'd learned—these most common individual problems, the ones that almost always led to common solutions, would work well as the basis to create a virtual training that would teach people how to solve their problems.

Within weeks, I had launched this virtual training group and sold eighty spots in one weekend. At $49 a pop, I had just made almost four thousand dollars, the equivalent of one month's worth of pay detailing cars. After only a month or two, I now had the confidence and cash flow to quit my full-time job.

I didn't run into Scott for another year. But when I did, I walked up, interrupted his conversation with someone, and told him what had happened. As a result of the idea he gave me, my business was now receiving 80 percent of its cash flow from virtual-training groups for the masses, and I was now making in a month what I used to make in a full year detailing cars.

It turns out that Scott was in the middle of interviewing someone who was considering joining an internship with his art business (@ colorpopart on IG), and I basically had just given the best in-person testimonial you could imagine. Since then, I've stayed in touch with Scott, and we now trade off business advice. And even though he's jealous of my hair, I'll always be jealous of his beard!

There are a few things I want you to get from this story. First, if you spend time listening to others, it always equips you to help more people solve problems. You'll regularly hear the problems that most people have in common, which will then allow you to create incredibly relevant material for your team.

I recently gave a leadership presentation at an event in Dallas called Platinum Edge. Afterward, I received a text from someone who had heard me speak a few years before. She said she was amazed at how much I had grown and how incredibly relevant my presentation was. What she didn't know was that I had just spent an extra two years listening to people and helping them find their own answers.

I'm always telling my friends that being a coach is the best career ever because people are paying me to listen. Of course, I'm helping them, but I'm also getting to learn from their problems and the solutions I help them find. It's cool to speak and give people answers, but it's way more profitable, for them and for you, if you take the time to listen. The result of listening is that you're on a constant journey of learning and continuing to be relevant.

Beautiful Data

The next thing I want you to realize is that listening turns you into the greatest salesperson you could possibly imagine. Why do I bring up sales in a leadership book? Because *leadership is sales*. Leadership is the ability to sell to someone else to do something. Whether that's selling them to work harder, selling them to stick with it, or selling them to have a better attitude, it's all sales. And when you spend your time listening to people, you start to accumulate stories and statistics that you can use to sell to people.

One of my favorite sales slogans says that people do business with people they know, like, and trust. Want to know the best way to get someone to know, like, and trust you? Be the person who's in their head. When I'm speaking on training calls, one of the greatest compliments I get is when people say, "OMG, it's like you're in my head!" What are they saying? They're saying that I hit the nail on the head. They're saying that I know exactly what they're going through. That creates trust.

Because I've spent so many hours listening to others, I have the ability to easily put myself in others' shoes. I have the ability to tell stories that everyone relates to. I have the ability to say things like, "I know for a fact that 90 percent of you think you work your business every day, when in reality, you mostly scroll your news feed and call it work. And then, you get upset when you don't get paid for it." Or "Your real problem isn't that you care too much about what others think; you just care too much about what the *wrong* people think. You're so worried about what people on IG and Facebook think about you that you aren't thinking about what your family thinks of you. You want to please others so badly you forgot that the reason you started this business was to make a better life for your family and make *them* proud."

I could go on and write an entire book using stories I've heard, over and over, that people use as excuses. And as a result, people trust me. Some people trust me because they've heard my name, and maybe they've heard stories from people I've helped. But for everyone else, I need to convince them that they can trust me. And the best way is to give them a tour of their own head.

Some people will join your team and will trust you because of your IG likes or your rank in the company. But for the rest of you who don't have large followings or any rank you wish to be said out loud, you'll need to earn that trust by listening and *collecting data*. And those of you who have everything going for you have probably found that no one on your team who's struggling really cares in the least about your IG following or rank. That may have sold them initially on joining your team, but now they're facing real life problems. And if anything, they use all of that against you by saying things like, "Well, I don't have a huge following like you" or "No one wants to sign up with me because I'm not ranked anything in the company." The very reason they joined your team is now the thing they use against you to convince themselves that you don't relate and can't help them. Sound familiar?

When you collect data and stats, you empower yourself to help people on a much deeper level. You give yourself the ability to make people feel that they can trust you, because you've been there. Maybe you're not currently there, but you *have* been there. And if you've been there and done that, and still came out on top, *that* is when people want your help!

CHAPTER 5
Leaders Relate and Duplicate

Maybe my favorite thing I do with my 1:1 clients is what I call the Breakdown Session. I created it in 2018, when I felt the coaching industry was starting to take advantage of people. In response, I wanted to be someone who was overdelivering a package, providing a higher level of value.

I'd seen the way some of my own clients had sabotaged their coaching sessions by constantly bringing up new problems, in order to avoid staying focused on the essential things their businesses needed. So I created a process that would guarantee we'd get down to what really mattered. Then we'd map out a full-blown plan to give us a structure to work from during our time together.

Typically, if you work with a true life coach, he or she will start every session with "What do you want to talk about today?" And personally, I think that's BS. The last thing I want to do when I pay someone a bunch of money is show up and then feel like I'm supposed to lead the process.

There may be times you find yourself working with a consultant who actually knows the subject matter, but who doesn't understand how effective coaching works. Instead of creating a structure that will help draw ideas out of you, that "coach" will charge you a bunch of money to teach you the exact system that individual found effective, assuming that same program will work for you. Also BS. Everyone has different goals, strengths, and paths, and needs to go through a process of self-discovery.

I created what I felt combined the best of both worlds. A structured system, but one that focuses on using questions to bring out and clarify learners' specific goals and strengths, while helping them to find *their* ways of getting there. Together, we define the primary goal(s). Then, we identify the main areas of focus needed to make those things happen. Next, I ask the question that everyone hates!

Up until this moment, it's been nothing but a fun and creative process. For the most part, we're defining things the trainees already know *how* to do but just haven't fully implemented to their potential. And then I ask, "What are some ways you can create *new* streams that will help you reach these goals?" That question is meant to take them outside the confines of what they already know, creating room to think creatively. Mostly, I've been challenging their focus, but now I'm opening a path to empower them to step into the shoes of a true entrepreneur.

Outreach by Franchise

Most network marketers are running their businesses like a local business. Remember the small church, local coffee shop, and local guitar stores I mentioned? Why are they still small? Because they're operating from what I call their *organic lid*. Meaning, they're getting the best results you can possibly get through *organic reach*. And if you're really good at it, you can hit some pretty big numbers that way. But you'll never achieve the kind of success and freedom you want, unless you start a franchise.

A franchise is your ability to leverage your time and presence by automating a system that will eventually work on its own. Yes, it likely will take a lot of time upfront—getting the paperwork, legal work, and other annoying parts of it taken care of. But then, when it's done, something magical happens. Once you roll out your new system, you can increase your income at *any point* by simply opening another location in a similar market somewhere else.

If I were to mention that my Facebook ad bot has conversations with 1600 people a month, and that my emails have reached inboxes more than a million times, and that, at any point, I can increase my income by simply increasing my spending, all of a sudden, I'd have your attention. But as I've said so many times, our limiting beliefs are constantly looking for a story to justify our fears and excuses.

Having asked them on this first call to think about what they really want to accomplish and watching them light up as they pondered it, now for the second time on this call, I watch my clients get excited as they envision the potential of creating some type of new income stream. Memories of all the podcasts and trainings they've heard flow through their imaginations—all the lovely things they learned about and previously ignored. Maybe they visualize creating a click funnel that would land people on their website, or writing that book that's long been sitting on the back burner. And then it happens. They run headlong into their limiting beliefs.

They realize the kind of work it will take, even if only on a subconscious level. They'll have to start from the bottom, and one thing high performers *hate* to do is feel like a newbie. No one ever just comes out and says, "You know, Josh, that sounds fun, but I'm really scared." No one ever tells the truth because their limiting beliefs are smart enough to play dirty.

Your inner "mean girl" will use your morality and love for others against you every time. So instead they say, "Josh, is that really relatable?" Or "I've considered that but it's just not duplicatable. I could never expect a new person to have a click funnel, and I don't want to be a bad example." So, let's talk about what it means to be *relatable*, and what it should look like to create a system that is *duplicatable*. Because this predictable response is taken sooooo far out of context.

Relatable and Duplicatable

First of all, for those of you *trying* to be relatable, the most relatable thing you can do is to continue to PUSH yourself to learn new things. Staying put is the least relatable thing in the world. When you're just doing the same things you've always done, you get comfortable. You get confused by your own success and start thinking that it's *easy*. You almost get offended by people who think it's hard and who struggle to put in the work and have success. But when you are constantly challenging yourself, you are faced with solving new problems every day, which keeps fresh in your mind what it was like to struggle with other parts of your business.

When your team tells you how they're struggling just to show up every day and try to do the things you now do naturally, you'll have a fresh story to tell them about how it's hard for you, too. You can be honest and let them know that you're also demanding even more of yourself and, at the same time, reminding yourself why it's so important to keep showing up. You become relatable when you *stay* in the trenches, *not* when you stand up on the parapet hollering down to everyone in the trenches.

"But here's the thing, Josh," (again in my best diva voice) "if my team sees that I'm running ads, or writing books, or doing a podcast, they'll think they have to do the same things to have success, and I would never want them to feel that way."

What if you were just honest instead? What if you told them about the hard work it took you to get from point A to point B, C, D, etc. And now, because of the hard work you've put in, you have this amazing opportunity to go after something even bigger. Because of the effort you put in to create a successful local business, you now have the freedom to create a franchise that will *work for you*. And it will keep on working behind the scenes—even when you're sleeping, vacationing, or I don't know, having more time to help them grow their local businesses.

Here's the thing, ***nothing*** we do as entrepreneurs is totally duplicatable. Think about it: 90 percent of your team is *never* going to show up every day. Does that mean you should stop showing up every day so you can be more "relatable"? Most of them will never rank advance, make money, quit their jobs, or build a dream life. But part of the reason we do those things is to inspire the people who *will* do those things.

If you want to authentically inspire others to reach their full potential, you have to resolve within yourself that you will *never* reach for anything less than your own full potential. Imagine how few people Oprah would have inspired if she'd never hosted her own talk show. Or Beyoncé, if she'd never taken over pop music. All of us are inspired by people who went BIG!

If you are doing anything less than what you're capable of, and using relatability as your excuse, you are only hurting the people who are following you and who would've gone to that next level *with* you. Not to mention the hundreds, if not thousands, of other people you *could've* reached if you *would've* written that book, created that funnel, or launched that podcast.

Sustainable

One more thing, if you're not willing to do the work it takes to build your "franchise," whatever that may look like for you, you're probably starting to get overwhelmed and exhausted by the work it takes just to show up and run the local biz every day. All the conversations, invites, and follow-ups begin to wear on you. The more you automate and outsource your business into duplicatable streams, the more you give your team HOPE that they can, one day, do the same.

No one wants to be a sales rep for the rest of their life. The reason we all do what we do is because we enjoy creating content, helping people, and making a difference. *Not* because we want to spend the rest of our lives glued to our inbox.

SECTION TWO

MOTIVATE

CHAPTER 6

Taking Control

This is where my type-A personalities are all shouting "AMEN!" My self-motivated, disciplined, hard workers are all cheering me on for this one. They will pound their fists during team calls and nod their heads along with me, because they think I'm talking to everyone else.

And because of the nature of the network-marketing industry, I usually am speaking to the unmotivated and excuse-making underperformers. But then, the leaders usually hire me to work with them in a more private 1:1 setting. In the initial consultation, they'll make sure to bring up all their credentials. They'll tell me how many months in a row they've hit the company's standard sales goal. They'll tell me how many years in a row they've achieved the company's "elite level" status—a level only two percent achieve.

"What is the biggest pain point in your business, right now?" I ask.

"Well, the problem is ... my team." They explain further: "Even though I provide a million resources, show up, and do all of my crap, they just don't seem to get it."

"What kind of goals do you have?" I ask.

"Well, that's the problem," they say. "I can't rank advance, if they won't work."

And then, they say my least favorite words in the world: "I'M NOT IN CONTROL!"

Here's what really pisses me off. This is someone who is incredibly self-motivated and, *supposedly*, never makes excuses. And then, when it comes to his or her *team*, all of a sudden this leader "can't control" the outcome.

Let's be honest, we've *never* had control. But if you've seen any success, it's because you made the decision to TAKE control! Think about it. Are you in control of whether people like or comment on your posts? No, but you've learned some tricks like asking them things such as "Dress A or Dress B for date night?" or "What's your favorite place to vacation?" You're not in control of whether someone follows your page, but you've learned techniques like following enough new people to get *some* of them to follow you back. You may run ads like I do, targeting people more likely to follow your page.

You *definitely* are not in control of how many people purchase from you or sign up for your team. But at some point, it dawned on you that if you just talked about your products and business enough (in a tactful way) and actually **asked** enough people to join you, a certain percentage (usually 10 percent) would eventually join you. You see, you were never in control. You were just determined enough to **learn** whatever you had to learn to find a way to get it done.

We've Only Just Begun

So, why is leading others any different? Why is it that we can watch YouTube videos and trainings all day if it means getting to 10K followers for the swipe-up feature, but aren't willing to put the same amount of work into learning how to Motivate and Mentor our teams?

I'll tell you why: you got LAZY! You thought the work was done. You worked so hard to get them to follow you, to like and comment on your pics, to show up for your special, virtual sneak peek or product party, and even worked your rear off to make sure they fell in love with the products so they'd become a "Lifer." The second they agreed to sign up as "business owners," you thought your work was done.

You've just spent the last six months of your life doing the amount of work it took to get that person to the place you wanted, and then you GAVE UP! Tell me, how is that leadership? Tell me why on earth do people get more value from you as your follower than they do as your business partner? The truth is that you have never been in control; you just found a way to take control until you got what you wanted. But you fell short. Why? Because you forgot that what you really wanted was a team full of leaders. And leaders aren't *found* nearly as often as they are *developed*.

You got confused because you are so self-motivated that you expect everyone else to be just as self-motivated. "I didn't need anyone to hold my hand, so why should I hold their hands?" you say. Well, first of all, you shouldn't hold anyone's hand. But neither should you abandon *your partners*, leaving them to figure out how to grow their own businesses, when the truth is that they may or may not bring the same natural talents to the table that you did.

Servant Leadership

If you want people who are 100 percent self-motivated, who do what they're told, and who don't make excuses, you'll need to change the way you do business. You'll need to recruit one person at a time. You'll need to put each through a lengthy application process, and then, a three-month trial period. You'll spend that three months teaching them the ins and outs of this business in person. Sounds horrible, doesn't it? Well, that's how companies in the corporate world recruit top-level people.

Last I checked, you started an online business to have more time and freedom, and to help *more* people not less. So if you want to continue recruiting people from around the world who have no credentials, no experience, and no formal training, ***they are going to need a little extra attention!***

This doesn't mean that you become their slave. In fact, I wrote this book specifically to help you understand what *servant leadership* is and what it isn't. And I'm going to be spending the next several chapters helping you understand how to motivate and mentor your team in a way that does *not* take all day and night, does *not* consist of all day 1:1 calls, and does *not* create a hand-holding environment.

I am going to teach you systems to train your people and create healthy boundaries that will give you more results in less time. But first I need you to understand something: What I have to teach you still demands that you go all-in, accepting the simple fact that getting someone to sign up does *not* equal a job done. It equals a job *begun*!

CHAPTER 7

The Boundaries of Motivate and Mentor

One of the greatest lessons I've learned about communication came from my high school theater teacher. I had somewhat of an identity crisis growing up. Though smart enough to have been a straight-A student, I let my longing for attention and social-time always take top priority. Imagine my excitement when I realized there was a class I could take that would enable me to get a good grade for acting up and role-playing fun characters!

Miss Dees was one of the more interesting teachers. If you met her, you would be amazed at her intelligence, enhanced by the way she carried herself with a sexy confidence. She was everything you would imagine a good actress being and was probably way too talented to be teaching theater and English to a bunch of punk kids like myself. I am grateful to have known her.

She once taught us that communication is just as much about explaining what something *isn't* as it is about explaining what something is. When it comes to leadership, we have hundreds of books telling us what leadership is, but so few examples describing what it isn't. Not surprising really that I find leader after leader completely overwhelmed and fatigued by what it takes to be a leader. People are spinning their wheels and burning the candle on both ends, trying to keep everyone motivated. So today, I want to teach you something that has saved my clients hours of time. This miracle cure has given them back their energy and passion to help others, and restored to them their personal lives!

Say it with me: BOUNDARIES!

This is probably the one word you've never read in a leadership book. You've been told to learn, grow, be humble, be flexible, communicate, stretch yourself, etc. These are all words that are constantly putting more and more on your plate. If you're not careful, you'll find yourself working so hard to serve and "lead" others that it all turns into a circus performance for which your team is the audience and you are the only act. So, I want to teach you a few things that will help you to understand what leadership *isn't*!

Know Your Own Value

When you set boundaries, you are telling your team, yourself, and your family, that your time and energy is valuable. Now, what is it that truly makes something valuable? Is it how available it is 24/7? Or is it how in demand it is because there's a limited quantity? If you don't have boundaries set, you are actually telling your team that your time is not valuable. No wonder they are demanding it all the time. No wonder they think it should be free. And no wonder they squander it so much. You can't put a trashy-wine price on your time and expect people to value it like Champagne. You must start by valuing your own time and energy.

Leadership is *not* being all things for all people. It is *not* giving everyone the same amount of attention. True leadership is valuing yourself and others enough to have boundaries.

Most leaders give very little time to their top performers because they're spending so much time trying to motivate and mentor people who are struggling. But if you're being clear-eyed, 80 to 90 percent of them are struggling because they don't show up. They're not asking you actual questions that need to be addressed; they're making excuses. Yet, you end up thinking it's your job to motivate them. You spend hours trying to help people figure out why they're not motivated, why they don't have time, why they can't seem to get their act together. In other words, you are not leading them, you are giving them free therapy. Last time I checked, you aren't qualified to give therapy, and you don't get paid to do therapy. Meanwhile, your top performers could be growing even faster, hitting even bigger numbers ... and making you even more money.

The 80/20 Rule

The 80/20 rule, also known as the Pareto principle, says that we get 80 percent of our results from 20 percent of our time. This is a global principle that applies to every industry, and even our own personal time.

Go study people working desk jobs, and you'll find that there is a small window of time in the day (20 percent) when they will accomplish 80 percent of their most important tasks. If you study the alcohol industry, you'll find that 20 percent of people pay for 80 percent of the profits. While I'm buying a six-pack that lasts me two or three weeks, someone else is buying a six-pack to consume tonight.

John Maxwell taught me this incredible trick (and many others have taught it as well). Find the few things in your business that bring you 80 percent of your results. Instead of giving them only 20 percent of your time, give them 80 percent. In doing so, you will quadruple your results without spending any extra time.

One of my favorite books of all time, *80/20 Sales and Marketing* by Perry Marshall, actually teaches you that there is a 20 percent to the 20 percent: If 20 percent of your people give you 80 percent of your results, then 20 percent of the 20 percent give you 80 percent of those results.

Okay, that may have been a little confusing. Let's pretend you have 100 people on your team. The 80/20 rule says that 20 of those people (20 percent) will deliver you 80 percent of your team's results, while the remaining 80 people contribute only 20 percent of the teams results. But if there is a top 20, that means that 20 percent of those people, or 4 people, are actually producing 80 percent of the top 20's results.

Here's the breakdown, assuming your team is responsible for $100,000/ year (just to keep the numbers easy):

- 100 people = $100,000 productivity, or approximately $1,000/person.
  - 80 of the people (the bottom 80) are responsible for only 20 percent of the results.
  - That means 80 people combine for $20,000 in sales, or $250/person.

  - 20 of the people (the top 20) are responsible for 80 percent of the results.
  - That means 20 people combine for $80,000 in sales, or $4,000 person.

  - 4 of the people (the top 20 percent of your top 20) are responsible for 64 percent of your results.
  - That means that 4 people combine for $64,000 in sales, or $16,000 person.

This was done based on sales, but you could just as easily do it based on your personal income, since your income is driven by your team's performance. In other words, if you make $100K/year, your top four people are responsible for $64K of it, and keep in mind that you may be one of those four, since you make your own sales and recruit as well. So, if you spend 80 percent of your day helping your bottom 80 performers, you are trading 80 percent of your time and energy for $20,000/year. While you are giving only 20 percent of your time to protecting your $80,000/ year.

A Dose of Reality

Let's go deeper, cuz I'm kind of a numbers nerd. I know my other numbers nerds are totally geeking out right now, and the rest of you have no idea what's happening, but this next step will make it all come together.

Let's pretend for a second that you work 30 hours/week to make $100K/year. If you work 52 weeks per year, you work a total of 1,560 hours per year. If 80 percent of your time is spent with your low-level performers, that would be 1,248 hours per year. And if your lower-level performers are only responsible for $20K of your income, that means you made $16/hr. for the time you spent with them. If you didn't already know, someone who makes $100K/year (based on 40 hours a week) makes around $48/hour. Eighty percent of your time, you are taking a $32/hour pay cut!

Consider this: The 20 percent of your time that you are spending with your top 20 performers is making you $80K/year. That means that you are making $80K/year for 312 hours, which is the equivalent of *six hours* per week at a rate of *$256/hour*! Here you are spending all this time learning a thousand IG tips and tricks, trying to figure out how to motivate unmotivated people, when you could increase your income $80K simply by working an extra SIX HOURS PER WEEK, spending time with the right people.

Here's what I really need you to understand. Every time you spend unnecessary time with low-level performers, you're making $16/hour when you could be making $256/hour. "But Josh, I'm not a selfish jerk. It's not all about the money." You're right, it's not. But for those of you who work a day job, I want you to imagine telling your significant other that you're about to give up 80 percent of your time to help people in need, while taking a $240/hour pay cut!

For those of you swimming in debt, struggling to make ends meet, or dreaming of taking your family on that dream vacation, go ahead and have this conversation with your family: The life you want for them, more than anything, is just a matter of spending time with different people. But you don't want to do that because there are eighty people sitting around and playing on their phones, instead of working. Those folks really need you to have a one-hour call with them to remind them to get over their damn selves and take a selfie for social media!

We're not talking about the difference between saving a starving child or selling a used car. We're talking about the difference between investing our time and energy into someone who is actually willing to WORK to make a difference in the world and someone who has the tools and refuses to pick them up and use them. This doesn't mean you're going to ignore the low-level performers. It doesn't mean you're going to cast them out of the village or stone them. It just means you are going to reserve 80 percent of your time for people who have earned it and 20 percent for people who are still finding their footing.

I have several chapters in which I will teach you how to make the most out of investing in *both*, not one or the other. I'll teach you how to work with your top performers in the Mentoring chapters. But first, a bit more on properly motivating people will be covered in the next few chapters. I'll show you how to motivate in a way that *empowers* people instead of enabling them. I just need you to understand how important it is to know the difference. To know and appreciate what's at stake.

YOUR FAMILY'S FUTURE IS ALWAYS AT STAKE! Your ability to impact the world with the resources you gain is always at stake. And the people who aren't ready to go to that level with you will still have *more than enough* tools to get there when they're ready.

Setting Appropriate Boundaries

This is why boundaries are so important. Every single day we are exerting an elaborate amount of time and energy. And the law of sowing and reaping says that we always reap a harvest on the seed we sow, IF it's planted in good ground. But if you're planting your seed on rocks, over and over, and expecting results, that's a problem. I'm going to teach you in the upcoming chapters how to use the Four Ms to set proper boundaries. And I really want to preface this by saying that boundaries do *not* devalue people. Valuing others *always* starts with valuing yourself first.

If you're finding yourself worn out, stressed, and deflated, why in the world would anyone want to join you? Or want to do what you do? Most of you are advertising some type of life of freedom. But is that something you even have? Or is that just something you say to sound good on IG? If people saw the way you currently work, would they have the urge to run in the other direction? I'm all about hard work. And I preach hard work. But if I'm worn out, exhausted, and unfulfilled, I have *nothing* to offer others.

I once heard someone say that if you're trying to talk to everyone, you're really not talking to anyone. There are a million trainings out there on speaking to your avatar and finding your niche. The point behind those is that if you are trying to be all things to all people, you're not really speaking as clearly and strongly to YOUR people. I say the same thing about leadership. If you're trying to help everyone, you're not really helping anyone.

You don't have enough to give to everyone. You have limited time and energy. But if you set boundaries and use the principles and systems I'm about to teach you, you can help more people than ever before, in less time, by simply focusing in on the right people.

Now that you understand what's at stake, let's talk a bit about what makes these two—motivating and mentoring—so different, and some of the common misunderstandings people have about them. Most people think that these two things are one and the same, but they are not. If you spend time mentoring people who need to be motivated, you'll waste so much time!

It's Your Team

Here's the best analogy I can give you. You are a recruiter, much like a college football team. Your job is to put together the best team you can to win the game. But you have to realize that everyone who shows up at the game is not on the team. Many of them are just fans. They love football, just like you. They love to win, just like you, but they aren't willing to show up for practice every day to earn a spot on the field.

They still contribute to the team in many ways. They buy tickets, which keeps the stadium open. They pay for snacks, drinks, and probably even some merchandise so they can wear the team colors. They cheer on the team and provide a ton of morale and energy. Without the fans, college football would not be what it is today. But let's not forget that the coaches and players are the ones who ultimately win or lose the game.

One of the biggest mistakes you may have made is assuming that everyone who joins your "team" is a player. You can call it a *team*, a *dominion*, or whatever you want. But when someone signs up under you, the leader of your team, it does *not* mean that new member is your starting quarterback or the future of the team.

To help you understand which lane people belong in—the motivate lane or the mentor lane—I want you to ask yourself whether an individual shows up to practice every day, puts in the work, and makes sacrifices to move forward, or just turns up to enjoy the "community," buy the products, and wear the merchandise. Naturally, this doesn't make this team fan any less of a person. But should you, as the head coach, spend just as much time with your biggest fan as you do with your team? Hell no! Even your biggest fans, the ones who buy tickets to sit on the sideline, don't get from you anywhere near the time and energy you give to your players.

Here is another analogy that will help you see who deserves your time: Think of these individuals as investments in the same way you think about investing your money. What's crazy to me is how much time and energy people will put into people they'd never invest their own money in. Sometimes when a client has a deadline for a specific goal that has a lot at risk and is trying to decide who to put their time into, I ask the following question. "If you had to invest your life savings in the success of only one of these people, and your future success depended on this one move, in which person would you invest the money?" Most of the time, it readily becomes clear. The place where you would put your money is the same place you should be putting your time and energy.

Now, this can be tricky because some people can fool us with their perceived potential. So, if my client still doesn't have a good answer, I present this situation. Imagine choosing between investing in two restaurants. Showing up at the first one, you find a nice, fancy sign and the place looks great! You walk in and notice the decor is very trendy and the workers are super friendly. But there are no customers, so you ask the owners what their marketing strategy looks like. They answer, "Well, we decorated the place, we change out the menus every week, and we really trust that if a few people come, they'll tell their friends and family about us. We don't know why it's not busier than it is; we've done everything we're supposed to do."

You go to restaurant number two. The sign is nice, but nothing special. You walk in, and find it clean and presentable, but not decorated nearly as trendily as the other spot. Not many customers here either. You ask the owners what their marketing strategy is. This answer is very different. "I understand that the only way to grow this place is to get the word out. I know we don't have the best location, but I hand out 500 flyers a day in nearby neighborhoods. We have punch cards to reward people for coming multiple times. We offer catering and advertise on all of the wedding and event sites. I'm a part of a local business owners' group where we strategize together, try to send customers each other's way, and give each other constant feedback on what we could be doing better. I'm doing everything I know to do, but am constantly looking for new ideas. As a partner, we would have open ears to any ideas you would have. We're here for the long haul, and willing to do the work it takes."

Notice both stores are having the same struggle: no customers. But if you had to bet your money on one or the other, would you bet your money on the trendy restaurant that's already done "everything I'm supposed to" or the restaurant that's not quite as pretty, but whose owners are working their tails off to get people in the door?

I don't know about you, but I'll invest in the one whose owners are putting in the work and have a growth mind-set over the trendier of the two—every time. Put your time and energy where you would put your money! Do *not* be tricked by people who have fancy IG accounts, but make excuses and have no work ethic. Anyone can look like an IG celebrity, but it takes WORK to grow a business.

To Motivate or Mentor?

You're going to have to learn how to stay in your lane. To know when you should be motivating and when you should be mentoring. Motivating is something we do for the masses. Everyone is invited. It's exciting. It's energetic. It is basically our "pep rally" mode. Hosting training calls, creating group challenges, and creating resources that help people find their place and start doing some of the most vital behaviors—that is motivating.

I teach my clients to create *team challenges*. In these thirty-day challenges, they pick something they want everyone to focus on. Maybe it's the company's minimum sales goal, maybe it's doing personal development. In my groups, I focus on recruiting challenges because I know it is the one thing every person needs to do that just isn't being recognized or celebrated enough.

You create a post every day asking people to check in when they've done whatever the challenge is. If it's a personal-development challenge, you could ask people to post a quote from their reading when they've read ten pages for the day. You make it exciting and you celebrate people for doing it. And then, you track how many days people are participating, and you follow through with weekly recognition and monthly prizes for those that are checking in the most.

Doing this one simple thing will open your eyes. You'll see, firsthand, a system that not only invites everyone to participate, but also boosts team morale, rewards people for showing up, and begins to show you who your PLAYERS are. The cream always rises to the top. You'll notice, in the first thirty days, which people have been actually putting in work and need your help getting to the next level, and which people have been doing nothing and just need your *attention*.

Of course, there are many other things that fit under the category of motivation. But the main thing you need to comprehend about motivating people is that, when you're in your motivating lane, you can have no emotional strings attached. You can't expect every person to want what you want. You can't get too frustrated when people don't show up. This doesn't mean that you water down the message of what it takes to get on the field; it just means you don't take it personally when people want to stay in the stands. And you certainly don't spend all your time trying to *convince* them to get on the field when, based on their work ethic, it's obvious they don't belong there.

Motivation is *not* convincing; it's inspiring. And it will be impossible to inspire anyone if your conversion rate is one percent. Let's be real—if you're trying to convince unmotivated people to show up for practice, your conversion rate will be one percent. So, you have to learn to let go. You have to learn to be just as inspiring for your "fans" in the stadium as you are for your Facebook and Instagram following.

When you learn to let go of the pressure of convincing others, you will find incredible power! You will find incredible confidence! And you will see that being a leader is nowhere near as hard as you have been making it. It is simple: Work with the working, and inspire the rest until they can show you that they want to be on the field more than they want to be drunk in the stands.

If this is where you feel stuck, I really want to help you. If you'll go to https://joshcoats.com/survey/ I have a separate survey to

help you to identify and pin point your struggles in motivating your team. If you'll take time to fill it out, I'd be happy to send you a free resource to help you to work on the specific struggle that you are facing! I want to equip you with every tool possible to help you to get your team moving in the right direction!

CHAPTER 8

Law of Energy

It's amazing how positive energy works.
Whether you have it or don't, people notice.

—Jon Gordon, *The Energy Bus*

In my virtual bootcamps, I work with a lot of people who are still working on finding their confidence. They sign up for my monthly groups because they lack systems and the motivation it takes to stay consistent in their business. I teach them this formula that Dave Ramsey talks about, and which I have made my own. Dave Ramsey says:

Consistency + Intensity + Time = Momentum

I add to it by saying:

Consistency + Intensity + (WORTH) + Time = Whatever You Want!

For an entire year, I ran small mastermind groups with people who were stuck at what I would call a mid-level. They were all hitting the company standards, but weren't rank advancing and weren't making the kind of money they wanted to make. I used a very simple structure with them (I'll teach you in the mentoring chapters) that had them tracking all their activities, but also included a weekly call where I got to dig in with them.

The number one lesson I learned from these groups is that people who are struggling to move forward in their business are almost always struggling with their own self-worth. Week after week, I would ask what they needed help with, and week after week, they would tell me about their self-doubts. The ones who stuck with me for six months or more saw their businesses EXPLODE as my belief began to rub off on them. As my friend and longest running client, Micah Folsom, always says, "Consistency breeds confidence."

As long as these people were able to get their focus and belief reset each week, they could then implement the right daily tasks for another week. It was almost like they were cars on a long road trip, needing to stop for gas once a week to get filled up. I can understand because I was the same way my first year in business. My bi-weekly calls with my mentor, Randy, were the one thing that kept me from quitting when things got hard.

When people finally get to the point that they find their own belief, something magical happens. I always say that the "light comes on." You begin to see an almost-literal light shine through their eyeballs! It's like the confidence and belief is glowing through them. You can see the actual complexion of their faces change. From that moment on, they have this thing that is more contagious than anything else you could imagine. It's called ENERGY!

The average American consumes 1.6 cups of coffee a day. I would say that I'm someone who definitely brings the average up! It is estimated that 68 percent of adolescents, 30 percent of adults, and 18 percent of children under the age of ten consume energy drinks (medicalnewstoday.com/articles/283929.php). Why is this? Because people are addicted to FEELING something. Nothing in the world feels better than energy.

Do you want to know what makes someone's business grow faster than any other single thing? Energy! Or as Dave Ramsey's formula calls it, *intensity*. When the right belief is mixed with the right intensity, you will see someone who is unstoppable! You could say:

Belief + Intensity = ENERGY.

When someone has this energy, I can help that person do just about anything with one simple tweak in focus. If you want to become a massive recruiter, simply shift your focus from selling products to recruiting. As long as you bring the same energy, you'll see recruiting take off in almost no time. But few people ever take the time to translate this same energy into their leadership.

Making It Work for You

The law of energy is something I've been dying to write about for some time now. John Maxwell has written about many laws in his books, *The 21 Irrefutable Laws of Leadership*, *The 15 Invaluable Laws of Growth*, and many others. But this law is MINE! The law of energy says that when energy is on your side, you can always outperform the statistics. When energy is not on your side, you'll struggle to perform even up to the statistics. Let me explain how this can work for you, and then I'll teach you how it applies to your leadership and team.

Most people in sales will agree that there is a 10 percent conversion rate. For every ten people you invite to try your product, one will purchase. That doesn't mean that if you send ten invitations today, you'll have a sale by the end of the day. It just means that if you invite ten every day, over time, one out of ten will convert. You have to remember that most sales take some back-and-forth and a few follow-ups. Your "one sale" from those initial ten invites may take as long as two or three months to come through.

Now I want you to imagine two people, each sending ten invites a day for their product. Let's pretend that the product is lipstick (shout-out to my SeneSisters). One of them—we'll call her Jessica—is on social media every day showing her life and her products, adding value, creating makeup tutorials. And she loves the products so much she can't shut up about them. Not in an annoying, every-post-is-about-my-products kind of a way. But in a genuine "I just 'effing' love-what-I-do" kind of a way!

The other one, we'll call Jane. Jane is confused. She loves the products, but feels awkward talking about them on social media. She doesn't want to come across as salesy, so she rarely mentions her products at all. In fact, she doesn't really like to show her own face on social media because it doesn't feel genuine to her. She shares pics of her kids, pets, and some different life events. But because she's diligent, she follows my daily tracker and starts up new conversations with at least twenty people a day and asks ten of them to try her products.

Now imagine the different kinds of responses these two people may get. Jessica is sometimes a little annoying, but she's also so full of life that people can't help but watch. When she goes to send someone a message, she's able to say something like, "Hey, how are you? I know this is super random, but you're always liking my posts, and I was just wondering if you'd ever thought about what I do. I'd love to give you some details, but if it's not for you, no worries at all! I just wanted to offer!"

Statistically speaking, six people will ignore the message altogether. Two of the four people who read it will say something like, "Thanks so much for thinking about me, but it's not really for me." The other two will both show interest, and one of them, after ten back-and-forths and a few videos, will end up signing up.

But here's the thing: Jessica is so present on social media, with so much energy, that even the nine people who either ignored her message or said no start to *notice* her even more. It's like when you buy a Chevy Tahoe and then start to notice that *everyone* has a Chevy Tahoe. Jessica's posts have always showed up in their feeds, but now they're more consciously aware of them. They start to notice how much fun Jessica is having doing this. They start to see how confident she's become and remember that this is not the same person they remember from a year ago. This is someone who seems to have something they've been missing for a long time: purpose.

Those nine people are watching every day. Two or three of them become so annoyed by Jessica that they become haters. They're watching from the background. They never like or comment on anything. But when she runs into them in person, they always make stabs at "your online business," so she knows they're watching. But the other six continue watching with curiosity.

When Jessica goes on a free trip with her company and posts pics with all of her "virtual friends," they notice. One woman, Miranda, even shows her husband some of the pics, hoping he gives some type of positive response. She really is curious about what Jessica is doing but doesn't want to bring up another "get rich quick" scheme to her husband. They still have $2,000 worth of products in the garage from the last three opportunities she bought into. To her surprise, her husband says, "I have a buddy at work. His wife is a part of that company. They're actually on that trip, too. I told him I was going to mention it to you. It seemed like something you might be in to."

Miranda is so excited she can hardly stand it! Her husband has bought in, just like that! She messages Jessica immediately. "Hey Jessica, sorry to bother you on your trip. But I was talking to my husband and we both think this could be a great opportunity. We haven't been able to afford a vacation in five years. I guess even if I never make any money and just get an annual vacation out of it, this would be worth it! How do I sign up?"

Boom. Jessica has now signed up two people from the ten she invited. And as the rest continue to watch, one or two more sign up over the next six months. This may not seem like a big deal, but because Jessica has consistently invited ten people a day to join her, and her *energy* is delivering her two to three new recruits for every ten she invites, her team is growing fast. Her confidence is growing just as fast! She starts closing even *more* people because of the growing confidence and belief that is showing up in her posts, messages, and life.

Remember Jane? We haven't seen her face on social media in several weeks. We know everything about her kids, but nothing about her. She can't start out with the same message as Jessica. She can't say, "Have you been curious about what I do?" because no one knows what she does. So, she has to talk about the only thing she seems to know how to talk about: her kids.

She messages twenty people a day to start up conversations about other people's kids. She gets a better response rate initially, because who doesn't love to talk about their kids. But it takes five or six messages just to get to that awkward place where she finally pulls the trigger: "I know this is super random. But I've been working this business from home that I really enjoy. Would you want to hear more about making money on the side?"

Here's the problem. Even if Jane sends this to ten people a day (just like Jessica did), it took her five or six back-and-forth messages just to get to this point. She is working so much harder than Jessica to try to get the same result. But because no one has seen Jane using or sharing her products, they know very little about her and have no idea what she's talking about; not surprising, her closing rate looks very different.

Even if she gets the same initial response—six people ignoring, two people interested, and one signing up—the long-term results look completely different. The nine who didn't sign up may still show some curiosity, but Jane's posts aren't in any way showing them what they're missing out on. There is no fomo (fear of missing out) whatsoever. They continue to see pics of Jane's kids and life events and *never once* think, "She's doing awesome things in her life; I'm going to reach back out and see what she's up to."

There are no long-term results to Jane's work. None. There is the one initial sale, and that's it. On top of that, because Jane doesn't have the same passion and excitement, she questions herself and whether she can even help the one person who is going to sign up. So, she doesn't properly follow up. She doesn't properly set expectations for how big of an opportunity this really is.

Rebecca, who has just signed up with Jane, has a major bill come up. Her husband's car breaks down, and they'll have to clean out their savings to get it fixed. Obviously, this would be the perfect time to have a side hustle that could help pay the bills. But because Jane hasn't painted a picture of this opportunity as something that can be life-changing, Rebecca doesn't even realize the money-making opportunity that's at hand. She returns all her products to get her money back and tells Jane that now isn't a good time. The one person Jane had is lost.

That is the power of the law of energy. When it's on your side, you become a fire-breathing dragon that the world stands no chance against! When it's not on your side, you sit around scratching your head trying to figure out what's wrong with you. Because everyone keeps saying things like, "If you want bigger results, you just have to do more work." But this sage advice doesn't seem to work for you. So you start to question whether you might be the exception to the rule. Trust me, *you* are not an exception to the rule; you just haven't worked hard enough on the *two things* that create contagious energy.

Belief + Intensity = ENERGY!

Your Best Friend or Your Worst Enemy—You Choose

Now let's talk about how this works with your leadership of your team. We'll continue with the same two people since you're probably relating to one or the other by now. Jessica is full of belief and showing up with intensity. She's growing her team and getting recognized left and right. But she has a serious problem. She's dynamite at recruiting people to join her team, but just can't seem to motivate anyone else to join in her enthusiasm. She gets on call after call with her team and is constantly frustrated by the lack of commitment from others.

She now has 100 team members, but only about fifteen of them show up for the weekly virtual-team training. The ones on the West Coast say the call is too early; the ones on the East Coast say it's too late. She moves to two calls a week so she can cater to both. One is a little earlier and one is a little later. It doesn't seem to matter. The same people show up, and the rest just come up with new excuses for why they can't make it.

Sally is a stay-at-home mom (#SAHM), so she's trying to get the kids fed. Susan works a full-time job, so she's picking up the kids from daycare (#twinmom) and is stuck in traffic. Mary doesn't have kids, but she has ten dogs (#petmom), and they need to be walked. Julia just got engaged (#engagedlife) and is spending the next twenty-seven years planning her big event. How can she get on a team training when she's still trying to figure out a good hashtag to use for their wedding and downing seven lattes a day at Starbucks trying to come up with their couple name (#powercouple)?

The lack of team commitment begins to weigh on Jessica. She starts to blame herself. "If I were a better leader," she tells her husband, "I would be able to motivate them." Her husband tells her how ridiculous this is. "You can lead a horse to the water, but you can't make it drink," he says barely looking up from the tv. He's now listened to Jessica complain about the same thing every night for two months. She's pretty sure his nightly advice comes from Googling "motivational quotes," which depresses her even more because her husband seems to be ten times more resourceful than her fellow mom bosses. Maybe he could speak on the next team call on how to use Google to find motivation.

Here's where the law of energy, which was on her side for the sake of recruiting, begins to work against her for the sake of leadership. She forgot the very simple lessons she learned from social media. Where did it all begin for her? She fell in love with the thing she was selling—and with her own journey. When she was posting all of IG about her life *and* products, she wasn't worried about who was responding and who wasn't. She was having the time of her life. One of the biggest mistakes I see people make is forgetting to have this same approach to leadership.

Please remember that leadership is still *selling*, just with a different product. If the number-one way to sell your products is to fall in love, make all the noise, and say "deuces" to the haters, then the number-one way to *lead* is to fall in love with the product (working your business), make ALL the noise, and say "deuces" to the haters—even when those haters are on your "team."

The problem is that you allowed yourself to think that, just because they're on your team, your work is done. You thought they were just as serious as you. You thought they'd be just as committed as you. You were wrong. When someone joins your team, the real work has just begun! Remember to treat your team like an extension of your social media. They are a group of people who decided to "follow" you at a higher level. So yes, you do have a higher level of influence with them, but there is still work to be done to turn *them* into influencers.

If Jessica doesn't change her attitude soon, her confidence will eventually get shot. The lack of energy will begin to trickle into her belief about recruiting. If she can't help people succeed, why would she, with a good conscience, continue recruiting people? She will either keep recruiting and feel disgusting on the inside, which will lead to burnout. Or she will stop recruiting altogether, which will lead to sticking around with zero fulfillment or eventually quitting.

This is one of the saddest things to me. Sometimes these people are able to make it to the top 2 percent of their company, but they get stuck at this very frustrating place. Everyone else thinks they're doing well. They still get a ton of recognition and make decent money. But they never create true freedom of time and money. I believe that nine out of ten people who actually put in the work to grow their business never go beyond the first rank advance, the one that most people can get by signing up one friend and maybe your mom or spouse. Most of you reading this have a spouse who is an unofficial rep!

But then, there are always a few more tiers on the way to the top. And at every rank, 90 percent get stuck, while 10 percent move onto the next rank. It's how we eventually get the 80/20 rule, and how there is even a 20 percent of the top 20 percent, and then, even another 20 percent. If Jessica isn't careful, she'll end up getting bitter and spending all her time looking for reasons and excuses that this business only works for the lucky ones. She'll begin to resent her company, and maybe even her upline and the top leaders. If she's not careful, she may become a poison to her own team, which she eventually spreads to others through chat threads, corporate events, and even groups that her own company put together to help her grow.

When people like Jessica come to me, they are either my easiest or hardest clients of all, depending on how soon in this negative spiral they come to me. If the frustrations have just begun, and they still have that momentum on their side, I can usually help them to flip the switch in the first call or two. I've had some clients come to me before the frustration turned into bitterness, who then went from making between $2K to $3K/month to making $8K to $10K/month in less than a year!

On the flip side, I've had others who have come to me much later. These are the hardest. Let me just say if you're someone who has become bitter and has allowed that to trickle into your team culture, it is NOT too late! You can ALWAYS change! But please don't get too wrapped up in everyone's favorite testimonials. You do not need a three- to six-month process; you need to spend a year with someone like myself, who understands the power of the law of process.

Law of Process

Taken from John Maxwell's *21 Irrefutable Laws of Leadership*, the *law of process* says that "A leader is not made in a day, but rather one day at a time." Something I've specialized in is helping people to embrace the process—a process I've personally endured twice. Once when I built my business the first time, which is something we've all had to deal with. But then, in year three of my business, I went through a divorce, and almost lost everything.

It took every scrap within me to recover the momentum and energy that was lost during my divorce. But I did it. For about six months, I hustled, sweat, and bled, with almost no tangible results. I doubted myself at every turn. I questioned whether I could do it again. I worried I had just got lucky the first time. I started to convince myself that everything I had built a career teaching was BS. And then, it happened. Out of nowhere, my numbers jumped.

I finally saw the results of the seed I had been sowing. The momentum was back. And after another six months of my building on that momentum, the ENERGY was finally back. I was breathing fire again, FEELING good about what I was doing, and making decisions with confidence again.

I will say that things have never been the same as they were pre-divorce. When you lose your momentum, sometimes you have to completely rebuild. In the process, you lose a lot of your lifers. You can still get caught up worrying that it's not as easy as it once was. It does something to you. The first build is exciting and full of adrenaline. Everyone is excited about you. Everyone is on your side. The second build is painful and can come with a lot of hurt and regret.

People who used to look up to you begin to look down at you. People who used to think the world of you sometimes want nothing to do with you. But you have to find a way to get over that. You have to find a way to count your blessings and just be grateful that you're back. And that you get to do what you love every day. You have to remember that you can't change the past, but you can build a future.

You have to use the wisdom of the experience to your advantage, and not worry about what it took from you. I may never have the spark I had at thirty, but my thirty-five-year-old self has gained wisdom and humility. I used to think that I was trying to build back up to Josh 1.0, but my coach, Ed DeCosta, helped me realize that I'm actually building Josh 2.0. We always have the ability to become a better version of ourselves—if we're committed to embracing the process and learning from our failures.

If you are Jessica in this story, please get help. Find someone who can reignite the fire in your soul. Make the decision to embrace whatever process it will take. You are still worthy. You are still capable. The only thing that has really changed is that you have a few more scars. I decided to wear my scars with pride. I used them as a steady fuel to prove that I was a fighter. I used every negative word that was spoken about me as a potent incentive, spurring me to make an even bigger difference. I made the decision to be the comeback kid and have a story that could impact even more people in even bigger ways.

Whether you are just getting started, or having to start over like I did, remember that Intensity + Belief = ENERGY! You don't have to be the most skilled, you just have to be the most determined. The law of energy is something that will change your life if you can get ahold of it. Unlike momentum, energy is contagious and can spread to others. It's never limited to just you. It's like a fire that, once lit, can spread through an entire forest and consume everything in its path. *Energy will be your best friend or your worst enemy, but the choice is yours!* Energy is one of the few things of which you always are in control.

I'm so happy to say that, even as I'm editing this book another six months down the road, I actually have a passion and fire like I've never had before. Josh 2.0 is complete, and I've been working on Josh 3.0! I am putting my original version to SHAME. Last month, we had record-breaking results, outperforming our previous best by almost $30K! I've teamed up with a few other people who are now operating under my umbrella, and have launched more groups than ever before. If you are someone in rebuilding mode, please shoot me a personal message at josh@joshcoats.com and tell me your story and what you're willing to do to create your 2.0 and beyond.

CHAPTER 9
Motivation Made Easy

John Maxwell is one of my favorite people on the planet because of how profoundly simple he is. The dude is like Yoda. He makes one statement that tells an entire story. While I have pages of notes from his teachings and books, there is one specific thing he's said, over and over, that probably gives me more respect for him than anything else. He has said that scholars and professors are always taking simple things and overcomplicating them to impress people. But *communicators* are always trying to take complicated things and make them simple to impact people.

What if I were to tell you that I am about to take what you've learned, add two more principles, and still make motivating your team simpler than it's ever been before? Now just to clarify, it won't be easy (that was just a catchy chapter title). But it will be SIMPLE! Nothing is easy. As I mentioned in an email to my subscribers today, as long as you are human or dealing with humans, life is never easy. If you're a parent (I have four kids), the struggle bus has just become a double-decker struggle bus! But please catch this principle: Systems take principles and turn them into intentional actions. And without intentional actions, all we've had is a good chat.

So, let's take the principles I've taught you—ownership and energy—mix them with a couple more, *recognition* and *measurement*, and turn them into one big motivational party. When you see how simple this is, you'll feel stupid for wasting so many precious hours exhausting yourself. It's okay, we've all been there, and we've all done that. But let's learn from it.

What gets celebrated gets repeated. What gets measured gets improved. These are two things my buddy, Kyle Sullivan, taught me. Kyle was the head of volunteers at a church here in Tulsa, Oklahoma. The church is called LifeChurch.TV, and it is spreading across the country at the rate of Starbucks in the early 2000s! In fact, every year John Maxwell does a leadership award at the annual John Maxwell Team training. (When I grew my business to doing over $400K in the third year, I envisioned myself, over and over, being called by John Maxwell onto the stage to win the award! Then I found out that the award wasn't limited to people on the JMT; it was presented to whichever person John Maxwell chose as an up-and-coming leader worldwide.) The pastor of Life Church, Craig Groeschel, ended up being the winner of the award. His church now has locations in ten different states. So, yeah, I wasn't quite on that level!

When I met with Kyle the first time, I found out pretty fast why Life Church is growing at such a rapid rate. Kyle, who is a product of Pastor Craig's environment, blew my mind. Here I was, a life coach who had built a business that had done $1.5 million in the previous three years, having my butt handed to me by a guy who oversees volunteers at a church. He made these two statements that I will never forget: "What gets celebrated gets repeated. What gets measured gets improved."

Kyle was on staff at the Jenks, Oklahoma, location. In his six months, he had grown the volunteer team from around 200 to over 500! If there are two things I trust, it's people who read as much as

I do and people who can show me RESULTS. This dude was both! He went line for line with me quoting my favorite authors such as J Max and Grant Cardone, while adding his own.

The Coach Also Gets Coached

I spent all of 2017 and 2018 revamping the structure of my groups and my 1:1s to make sure everything was performance-based. So of course, I agreed 100 percent with the statement "What gets measured gets improved." In my 1:1s, I make my clients report their numbers at the beginning of every single call. This is forcing them to continually measure so that they are subconsciously wired to improve those numbers.

Let's talk about this first. If you want people to improve, you've *got* to have regular measurements. This can include monthly, weekly, and daily recognition for numbers produced, but I believe it needs to go a step further. We also need to measure ACTION.

Before I ask my clients to report their numbers, I ask them to rate their action level on a scale of one to ten, and then I ask them to rate their energy level on a scale of one to ten. What am I doing? I'm trying to train them to consider their action and energy as more important than their results. Results can fluctuate depending on market trends. But show me someone whose action and energy is a ten out of ten, week after week, and I will show you someone who will have success regardless.

But I made a huge error during my 2017–18 revamp. On my quest for creating a performance environment, I left out one of the main ingredients. My first couple of years of training others had been all about creating an environment of energy and community. When I decided that people needed a higher level of accountability, I made the mistake of using *or* instead of ***and***.

Grant Cardone teaches that anytime you put yourself in an "or" situation instead of an "and" situation, you miss it. This one simple thing has helped me on countless calls with clients. People want to know whether they should push for large numbers OR focus on a better customer experience. My response: "Why are you trying to do *or* when *and* is an option?"

Well, sometimes, the coach needs to be coached. When Kyle told me, "What gets celebrated gets repeated," I was shaken. My soul was shaken. I left that meeting and allowed that one phrase to soak for several months before I knew what to do with it. I knew that I had missed it. I knew that I'd let go of the excitement and energy in my groups to create this high level of performance training, which was actually hindering the performance of my groups. I was maximizing on calling out people for *not* doing their work (which they did need), but I was minimizing the celebration of people actually doing their work. I had thrown out the baby with the water. Damn.

In January of 2019, I invited Kyle to come meet with my team. My new focus for all my groups was to insert this one word into my groups: ENGAGE! I knew that, if we wanted to really help people, we had to take time to engage them in conversation and make them feel celebrated. I sometimes say that my groups are like a "30-day bootcamp for your biz." But what I clearly needed was for the participants to feel part of a COMMUNITY, or a brotherhood/ sisterhood, not just a drill team.

Kyle sat down with us and ran the numbers on our "bootcamps" to help us to see that the turnover in our groups had an 85 percent turnaround rate. In other words, even though people **needed** the bootcamp, by my having provided the drill sergeant without the fellowship, 85 percent of attendees didn't see enough value to stick around more than one month. Even though my group had 90-plus percent of people doing their work, which is an incredible stat, they weren't sticking around. Therefore, they weren't seeing success, and we were losing precious customers that should've become testimonials. Without a brotherhood/sisterhood, no one can endure the grit and pain of the bootcamp, no matter how good of a drill sergeant you are.

Your Toolbox

So let's put together all of our motivational tools, and meld them into a duplicatable system that doesn't take up all your time. We know we can't have any strings attached. We have to pour belief into others without an exact expectation. We know we have to have ENERGY on our side, which is a combination or our worth and our intensity, applied consistently over time. We know we have to celebrate the things we want people to repeat and measure, the things we want them to improve. So, let me show you how I do ALL of that in one! Here is my game plan used in the main group I run for the masses (the PUSH Mastermind).

PUSH Mastermind Game Plan

Weekly Call: This allows me, once a week, to bring my ENERGY and belief, and pour it into the group. Ninety percent of what I teach is the Consistency + Intensity + (WORTH) + Time formula. I usually speak for thirty to forty minutes, mostly because I love to speak, and then I answer any questions people have from a thread we post. I've found that answering questions once a week is more about giving people the affirmation they need that they're on the right path and they just need more time. Of course, people ask all kinds of questions from "How do I close the sale?" to "How often do I follow up?" But the main thing is that sometimes people who are struggling with their worth just need someone to give them a solid answer they can put their confidence in.

Monthly Challenge: Every month, I come up with one to two things I really want people to focus on. And then, I create a challenge to "celebrate" the thing I want them to repeat. I choose to do challenges around recruiting because I know that it's the number one thing most people don't do, and *no one* seems to be emphasizing it enough. But to make it fun, I don't just celebrate when people get a recruit. I have them on a tracker inviting several people a day, and I celebrate both the yeses *and* the noes they get. Remember, you have to get a lot of noes to eventually get a yes. So, we should *celebrate the action* and not just the results.

Every day, there is some type of check-in that says something like, "Hope you crushed it today! It's time for the daily check-in! Comment below showing how many people you recruited today and how many NOES you got!"

Weekly Recognition: Every Friday, we ask people to comment below with their biggest wins of the week. This gives them a chance to brag on themselves and to remember that they DID have some wins, even if they didn't make any sales or get any new recruits. Then I take two to three of my personal favorites and give them a shout-out on the weekly call.

Monthly Celebration: At the end of the month, I ask everyone to share a full-blown testimonial of the success they've seen that month. I pick two winners that I call my Rock Stars of the Month. One is for the person who recruited the most people. I always want to recognize the one at the top to encourage that high-performer to keep performing. But I also choose one person who had the biggest business *improvement* that month. I, personally, believe that being performance-focused means we have to celebrate what we really want. And the thing I want most is not necessarily for anyone to be the top performer—I just want them all to improve.

Creating a culture that says "Jessica's success is the only success that counts or matters" is *not* what I am after. What I want people to know is that I'm constantly looking for people who are improving and reaching toward realizing their full potential! A quote I created for an IG post, one time, says: "Why would you settle for being the next version of someone else when being the best version of yourself is always an option?"

I want people to know that becoming the best version of themselves is enough. I don't need everyone on my basketball team to score thirty points per game; I just need everyone to perform at a level of personal best. When we all perform at our best, we win every time! But that will look different for every player on the team.

Ordinary Systems Lead to Extraordinary Results

Michael Gerber says: "Systems allow ordinary people to achieve extraordinary results predictably. However, without a system even extraordinary people find it hard to predictably achieve ordinary results."

I've mentored some pretty extraordinary people in the last five years. Some of these leaders made as much as seven figures a year running a business on social media. Some of them have downlines as large as ten thousand and beyond. But the one thing that can stunt the growth of anyone is not having a system in place.

When I teach people my system for motivating their team, they're usually shocked at how simple it really is. If you take the time to implement this very straightforward system, you'll find yourself lighting a fire in your team in about two to three hours per week. And if this system doesn't fan the flames, it's possible you just haven't *modeled* enough to have anyone to light up. If that's the case, thank GOD, you now have a system that only takes two to three hours a week. When the right people do come along, you'll have a system in place, ready to engage and celebrate them!

You now have a system in place to motivate people, using less of your time and energy. You've just opened up the time you need to start properly mentoring your team. You finally have the brain capacity to really lean in with your top workers, your "80-percent" producers. You can, at long last, enjoy the work that you have to do as a leader. And know this: The beautiful thing is that I'm going to teach you the principles of *properly* mentoring, which you will find takes even less time than you imagined and gets you more results than you've had!

SECTION THREE

MENTOR

CHAPTER 10

Work with the Working

"Here's the thing Josh, I have this handful of folks on my team that say they really want to do this. Like they want it so bad. They'll get super excited for a few weeks, but then won't follow through. I've tried digging into their why. I've tried helping them find their limiting beliefs. But they won't do the tasks that I give them, and as a result, their business isn't moving forward."

This is a pretty common question that I get: "How do I help the ones who say they want it, but don't put in the work it takes?" In fact, probably every leadership call I've ever done that I allowed for Q&A time at the end has brought up this scenario. There seems to be this strange place where people get stuck.

So, I'm so glad you asked. This is my favorite issue to address and one of the main reasons I wrote this book. The whole book has been leading up to this moment, when I can help you to set the *most important boundary* in your business. We have a lot to talk about because there are so many things at work here.

First, let me help you first understand yourself. One of the crucial things you can do as a leader is to become *self-aware*. Because if the problem is internal, we can change all of the external things, and it won't matter. We have to go inside first.

Four Personality Types

Society is made up of four different types of people. While some personality teachings go much deeper into the wiring of humans to come up with nine or more personality types (my favorite to study is the Enneagram), I'm going to teach you the main method I use for teaching my clients, because it makes things simple. If it's not simple, you won't remember it and will probably struggle to remember what personality type anyone is, other than yourself. While I love deeper studies like the Enneagram, they aren't as beneficial for simplicity in understanding the masses.

I'm going to teach you my *animal types*. This comes from a presentation I heard at a mandatory staff meeting during my auto-detailing days. The owner loved to help out friends, and he had a friend who did team-building exercises. He made a Saturday training mandatory, asking all of us to come in and do a workshop. To this day, I don't remember anything else this person taught us, or even his name. I feel a little bad about not knowing his name, since I've retaught his lesson over and over.

Five years later, I was on a call with a client who was struggling to help someone she was mentoring. She mentioned how this specific mentee really struggled with all of the talk about numbers and sales because she cared more about helping people and felt all of the numbers talk was icky. I said, "Well, that's easy; you're a rhino and she's a retriever. No wonder you're struggling to help her; you don't understand her language." I, then, proceeded to teach her what I'm about to teach you, and she was so blown away that she couldn't believe I hadn't already taught this in any of my courses.

Actually, I was thrown off by my own response because I didn't even realize I had remembered these animal types until this conversation came up. Apparently, this teaching was so simple and had made such an impact on me that I subconsciously stored the information without even realizing it. That's when I knew I had to teach it. Clearly, anything that can be remembered for five years without any effort is something that can be an effective tool. So, prepare to have your mind blown!

Humans have four basic personality types: the rhino, the peacock, the golden retriever, and the owl. A combination of two simple things determines which category applies to you: You are either more outgoing or more reserved. And you are either more task-oriented or more people-oriented. With those binary descriptions of how you relate to the world, your personality type can be sorted into being represented by one of these four animals. While everyone has a primary and secondary animal, this teaching is about keeping things simple so you can understand yourself and others.

The rhino is outgoing and task-oriented. Most people think rhinos are extroverted because they tend to show a higher energy, are usually confident, and are usually fun in social settings. But they are actually wired more like introverts. While they are fun and good with people, they can only handle being in groups for so much time before they need to get away and recharge.

Rhinos worry more about the task at hand than the person they are talking to. Rhinos have learned social skills because of the need to connect for the sake of accomplishing their tasks, not necessarily because they enjoy socializing. The rhino is usually self-motivated, competitive, goal-oriented, and confident in demeanor. The rhino theme is "Join me or get out of my way!"

A high percentage of top leaders in the industry are rhinos, simply because they are willing to do the work it takes to succeed. When it comes to being an entrepreneur, we all can learn from the determination of a rhino. But rhinos' greatest weaknesses are that they get drained by others, show little sympathy for others who don't catch on as quickly as they do, and usually struggle to see the highest level of success unless they learn how to become more aware of the needs of others.

The peacock is outgoing and people-oriented (this is my primary animal). Like the rhino, peacocks are good in social settings and carry on conversation without struggle. Where rhinos talk to people because it's part of the agenda and because they know they need to make connections to succeed, peacocks are doing it because of the pleasure they absorb getting attention. The peacock's motto is "Give me the spotlight … ALL OF IT!"

Peacocks love to be the center of attention. They love to make people laugh and are usually willing to make an ass of themselves as long as it gets attention. The class clown, the drama queen, the fashionista, and probably a self-proclaimed mermaid—all are peacocks. They show up to the party twenty minutes late, because nothing fun happens in the first twenty minutes, not to mention that they changed clothes ten times to find the outfit that felt perfect for the occasion!

Peacocks have a huge advantage when it comes to social branding and attraction marketing; it's like getting paid to do what they do anyway—shine the spotlight. But they also are so inept at completing tasks that sometimes they forget to do any of the stuff that matters. They'll spend seven hours making graphics for their stories and forget to respond to their messages.

The golden retriever is reserved and people-oriented. Like peacocks, they love to be around people. They love to be where the party is and feel like they're a part of everything. But they hate the spotlight. They are there for the community. They love to feel like they are part of a specific mission that is benefiting others.

While the peacock is busy entertaining everyone, the golden retriever is probably making sure everyone has a drink. The golden retriever is probably the designated driver because, in wanting everyone else to have a good time, the golden retriever is more than willing to sacrifice his or her own fun for the sake of the group of friends. So everyone else can get home safely, the golden retriever wants to stay sober.

Golden retrievers, at their best, serve others, care for others, and are the most loyal friends you'll ever find. They will listen for as long as you need to talk and would fly across the country to help you in need. But at their worst, they become people-pleasers who don't know how to say no. They find themselves serving everyone else in hopes that someone will notice, and when no one does, they start to become very bitter on the inside.

Their biggest problem is they'll never tell anyone they're bitter because they don't want to upset anyone or burden them with their problems. At their worst, golden retrievers can be the hardest of anyone for me to help succeed in a sales-based business. But when golden retrievers can learn self-motivation and boundaries, they have the ability to supersede all the rest of us because of their genuine belief in and care for others. A golden retriever who learns to develop some rhino qualities can become virtually unstoppable.

The owl is reserved and task-oriented. I put the owl last on purpose, since it's my exact opposite. Owls are the first to arrive and the first to leave. They are at the party only because their spouse dragged them in. They love to organize everything. Everything has a system that ensures things are done in the best way possible. The world is black and white. They research every decision they make so that they can make sure they always make the best choice.

You will never win an argument with an owl, because that owl has done more research than you, knows more facts than you, and wouldn't have this opinion unless it was the right one. The owl's philosophy is, "It's not an opinion; it's fact." They tend to believe that their way is the only way. They are very logical and don't tend to show emotion, other than passion. They are extremely passionate about what they believe is right. If owls believe in something, it's because they've checked their facts, and they will fight for it at any cost.

The hardest part of this business for an owl is that there are *no exact formulas for success* in entrepreneurship. One of my favorite teachings is to compare business to riding a bike. You can study the bike all day long, but nothing really makes sense until you jump on and give it a try. As a peacock, I know firsthand that's how we live life. We jump on everything and try because we are thrill-chasers. Even if we fall off the bike, we'll have a fun story to tell. Also, we'll have had someone record it so we could show everyone.

Owls struggles with this concept. They will study the bike for a year, only to realize they still don't understand how to ride it, which means there must be some other resource they haven't found yet, so they keep researching. *If* an owl can learn how to just jump on and ride, incredible success will follow because of that ability to streamline every experience into efficient and duplicatable systems that are easy to teach.

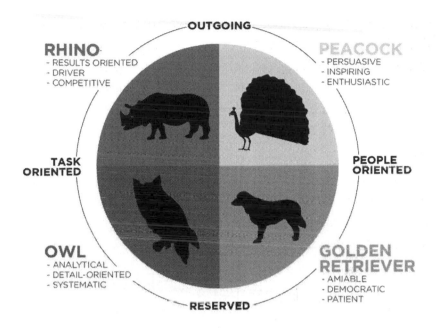

Task-Oriented / People-Oriented

I taught you all of that for two very specific reasons. (1) For the sake of this chapter, more than anything else, I want you to understand the differences between *task-oriented* and *people-oriented* human beings. At one of my John Maxwell trainings, Dr. Robert Rohm taught us the DISC personality types, which is the exact same concept as the animal types I teach, but with different names. You can go to 123test.com to take a DISC test, and then you just have to do this simple translation:

The D (Dominance) is the rhino.

The I (Influence) is the peacock.

The S (Steadiness) is the golden retriever.

The C (...) is the owl.

Notice how much the owl is my opposite? I don't even remember what the C stands for! I obviously could've Googled it, but once I typed it up and realized I had no idea what the C stood for, I laughed a little and just left it. I'm sure it stands for *Closer to God*, or *Currently researching so I can win the next argument with Josh*. Maybe it just stands for *C, I told you I was right!*

Dr. Rohm told us that approximately 80 percent of the world's population are people-oriented (peacocks or retrievers), and only 20 percent, task-oriented. Being a peacock himself, he then joked at what a harsh place the planet would be if 80 percent were task-oriented and only 20 percent, people-oriented! But think about it, the coffee shop that I'm currently sitting in (Holla! Cirque Coffee Libations) has anywhere from eight to ten employees that are baristas who must also serve the customers. While we often refer to baristas as artists, they really are more people-oriented. They have to learn the craft of making drinks, but the real art is done by the people who are roasting the beans.

Bean roasting is the art that only a few people even know how to do. The roaster is in a different room, all by himself, working all day on perfecting the bean. He doesn't have to talk to others, doesn't have to explain what he's doing to anyone. He just researches the absolute best way to do it and then does it. He is the owl of the operation. If the business is successful at all (this one is), there's a rhino somewhere running around like a chicken with her head cut off, talking to vendors, training employees, pushing events, and acting as the backbone of the workload.

The roaster (owl) without the rhino (manager) will rarely succeed. But imagine if they were to hire a bunch of owls or rhinos to serve the customers? These baristas are the golden retrievers and peacocks, who enjoy the environment of serving and helping people. The retrievers are probably doing most of the dishes while the peacocks are having twenty-minute conversations with their favorite customers, and it is safe to say the people-oriented employees are a must.

This means that 80 percent of the people reading this book are people-oriented. I'm going to address you first, because you struggle with boundaries more than anyone. You are usually one or both of the following: people pleasers or people saviors. Then I'll address the task-oriented, who set boundaries a little *too* well!

People-Oriented Types

To my fellow **people-pleasers**: Yes, I am a people pleaser, too. I get it. I feel you, hear you, and understand you! And I wrote this book for you. If you are like me and grew up in a religious culture, you are extra screwed up, because as I've said so many times, our limiting beliefs are constantly looking for a story to justify our fears and excuses. As humans we are constantly looking for confirmation of our own limits. When you mix religion with that, it becomes an incredibly strong hold that takes even more perseverance to work through. Nothing could be more concrete than thinking that God (the Universe, etc.) wants you to do things a certain way.

We take our religious beliefs like "Love your neighbor as yourself," and mix them into our business practices. We also take our religious values and mix them into our business values. If you've been taught by your religion to treat people as equals, regardless of their background, you'll think that you have to treat everyone in your business the same. And I get where you're coming from, but let me explain to you how out of context this thinking is. I'm assuming you have some people who are close to you. People you consider your best friends. If they call you in the middle of the night with an emergency, you would drop everything you're doing to help them.

What if a stranger called you in the middle of the night? Would you do the same for that person?

Another question. Imagine your best friend needs someone to watch the kids tonight, last minute, because something incredibly important has come up, and no one else is available. You probably are more than happy to help out. What if a random person at Target tells you that something urgent has come up and is wondering whether you could watch their kids? Same answer?

You see, loving your neighbor as yourself is a principle, not a mandate. The point of the proverb is to challenge us to VIEW all humans as equals, which will alter the attitude we have toward others, and therefore, alter our actions toward others. No one in their right mind goes walking through Target actually treating every single kid like their own. You would go broke! Do you see how we take principles that we use every day with common sense, and then, pervert them to cripple ourselves in other areas like our business?

When people message you at 9:00 p.m. asking you a question that you know they could have had answered on Google, you instantly hear Jesus in your head saying, "Love your neighbor as yourself." What's funny is that, if Jesus could actually walk into your living room and sit down next to you, he would probably say, "Put your phone down and pay attention to your family!" In trying to "serve" all people equally, you forget to include your own family on that list.

Can I go one step further? Of course, I can: It's my book, and you already paid! You also forgot to include *yourself* on the list. You can't possibly love your neighbor *as yourself* if you aren't treating yourself with love. And if you are spending all your time trying to "save" everyone else, then you are "losing your soul to gain the world." Which leads me to my "**people-saviors**."

Because I work with a lot of people who come from religious backgrounds, and people who generally want to serve others, I find myself in conversations with my clients that sound something like this: "Josh, here's my struggle. I genuinely love and care about my people. I really believe in them and find it hard to pull myself away from them, even when I know I should. I feel like, if they just keep getting access to me, maybe they'll come around."

And I have to tell them this: "You are not anyone's savior!" To think that you are somehow powerful enough to fix someone is to think a little too much of yourself. One thing we constantly forget is that others have this thing called FREE WILL! It's called *free will* for a reason. It's everyone's born-right to become the person that individual wants to become.

We need to understand that everyone doesn't *want* to become the person we want them to become. They don't always even want to become the person that they want to become. Lots of people want to lose weight. So how is it possible that there are so many people who are overweight? Because some of us enjoy our tacos more than we enjoy six-pack abs. It doesn't mean that people don't have a desire to change; it's just that their desire to stay the same is stronger.

So, what do we do with people who have a stronger desire to stay the same than they have to change? We keep them in our motivation lane! We keep showing up on trainings and resources that we're creating for the masses. Our job is to continually point out the benefits of changing and remind them of the rewards down the road, while being honest about the work it will take. But if people prove to us over and over that their desire to change is weak, we should not be giving them our 1:1 time over and over. When we think we can save people, we usually end up enabling people.

Imagine your kids are coming to you repeatedly asking for money for the same thing. Each time, you tell them they need to clean their rooms if they want an allowance. Over time, they never get around to it, and yet you end up giving them their allowance anyway. What would you be teaching them? That they can get what they want in life without working for it. What a detrimental lesson to teach!

Whenever we try to play the role of a savior instead of the role of a mentor, we send that message. We're telling people they don't have to work to get our time and energy. In fact, we're actually teaching them that the way to get our time and energy is to come up with questions about problems that they haven't put any work of their own into resolving. We're literally breeding needy followers, instead of raising up leaders.

Task-Oriented Types

Now let's talk about those of you who are task-oriented. For my rhinos and owls, you haven't related to a single thing I just said about pleasing and saving people. That's never been your struggle. You don't like excuses and you don't listen to excuses! You distance yourself from people without even trying. You're already drained enough by others; you definitely aren't giving your time to people who whine and complain all the time. Here's what you need to learn: grace! While I don't want you to turn into a people-pleaser, you're going to need to work on giving people a little time and space to figure things out.

While the peacocks and retrievers give people too much grace, allowing them chance after chance, sometimes the rhinos and owls don't give anyone a chance at all. Because you are so task-oriented, you always get the tasks done. You do not leave the office without checking every box. And especially for my rhinos, you are usually seeing positive results because of this. But you can't look at others' numbers and assume they are lazy if they aren't getting the same results.

You need to remember that there are *many* things working for and against each person based on their personality type, natural strengths, and self-esteem. While you need to hold people to a standard of actions, I don't, personally, believe in holding everyone to a standard of results. I believe there is a time and place for that, but it's usually at higher levels. For example, in my training group, the PUSH Mastermind, the focus of the group is reaching the masses. The point is to help **anyone** who wants to move forward in their business. So, there aren't any specific results required to be in the group. But you do have to live according to my activities tracker, or you get kicked out!

For smaller groups, often I impose a minimum sales number to qualify for the group. This prerequisite ensures that I have people coming together who are on similar playing fields. This leveling of proven abilities allows them to all feed off each other and learn from each other. It also makes sure that when I answer one question for the group, my response actually applies to everyone else in the group. It saves them time because they don't have to listen to answers that don't apply to their business. It saves me time because I don't have to answer more than a few questions, since they all have the same couple of questions.

Filling Your Stadium

Let me share one more analogy that I think will help you fully grasp the significance of working with the working. Pretend you are the coach of a football team. Some of you love sports, and some of you are more like my girlfriend, who is kind enough to put on whatever shirt I ask her to wear to support my team. Either way, I think you'll all understand this sports analogy.

On your football team, you have eleven people who have to be on the field in order for you to play. Any fewer, and you'll get a penalty and the game can't even be played because each player has a different role; they take on different positions based on size, strength, speed, and individual skills. But every position is just as important as the others, even if only one or two of the positions score most of the points and get the majority of the credit.

But then, you also have several people on the bench. You really need to have at least one person on reserve for each position on the field in case someone gets hurt. But best-case scenario, you have two people on the bench for each position. The second-string, or the second-best players at the position, still play throughout the game, when the ones who started need a breather. If something happens to the starters or the second-string, the third-string players need to be ready to go at all times.

Between our starters, our second-string, and our third-string, we now have thirty-three players needed, and that's just for offense. We need an additional thirty-three players for defense. We won't get into *special teams* to keep this simple for my "sports" fans. As a leader on your team, you have probably thought about your starters, maybe even your backups, but here's something you may well have forgotten about: You also have to fill a stadium!

As a business owner, you aren't just the coach, you're also the owner, the marketing team, and the sales director! We use terms like team, dominion, and downline, but in reality, we have more than just a team full of players to work with, we have an organization to run. Imagine, what would a football game be without any fans?

The football stadium is made up of a wide range of people. There are people who go to only one game a year. People who go to every game when the team is winning and zero games when the team is losing. People who have season tickets and show up shirtless even when it's snowing. And others that we don't even know are there because they're in a fancy booth they paid $5K for, so they wouldn't have to sit next to the hairy-chested guy with his shirt off!

I always teach people that recruiting really is no different than selling; it's just a different package. And here's where that is really going to make sense for you. If we were to remove words like *team*, *downline*, *rep*, and *recruit*, we would see that EVERYONE is either a *customer* or a *producer*. People are either producing results for the team (players) or they are customers.

The customers are still a very important part of the game. Without them, none of us have a job. But to pretend someone who sits on the front row of every game with a painted chest is going to somehow win the game for you is CRAZY! Thank God for that crazy guy; he's the reason we all love to play. But I'm not giving him the ball with ten seconds left when we're down by six. And if I'm not going to give him the ball, or put him on the field, why would I invite him to practice and spend my time and energy trying to teach him how to catch a ball?

Now, that does *not* devalue him. It just means I'm using wisdom to run my organization to make sure the team wins. *Because when the team wins, everyone wins!* That guy with his chest painted has the best day of his life when the team wins, and he doesn't care that someone else got the touchdown. He will leave, go to the bar down the street, and say with pride, "WE WON TODAY!" He still sees himself as part of the team, even if he's not on the roster. And he loves his part on the team!

Sometimes, I think we do more damage than good when we take people who really just want to cheer on the sidelines, or travel with the team on the bus as a water girl/boy or cheerleader, and try to turn them into the starting quarterback. The guy on the front row has dreamed about being the starting quarterback since he was six. He still plays the scenario out in his living room after the game. But he didn't want to practice every day. He didn't want to work out at six in the morning. He didn't want to go to summer camp when the other kids were sleeping in. He may have the same dream, but he wasn't willing to do the work. And he's okay with that. He's okay with being the best fan ever, and he still makes it onto SportsCenter occasionally, when the running back jumps into the stands to high-five him after scoring a touchdown!

You've Just Gotta Show up for Practice

Let me offer one more thing you need to consider when choosing who to put your time and energy into. I have clients who constantly overvalue the stats of last season. In most companies, there is a specific rank where the company recognizes someone as a leader. Usually, it means you have eight to ten people you've recruited, and so the company recognizes you as having a team. For a lot of my clients, advancing to their next rank depends on getting their own people to that leadership rank.

To make things easy to understand, I'll use a really simple example. One of the companies I do a lot of work with has a rank called *Diamond*. This means you have eight recruits under you (and a few other technicalities we won't talk about here). If you are a diamond, and help someone under you go diamond, you become a one-star diamond. For every person you help get to diamond, you get another star. At two-star, five-star, and fifteen-star, you get extra bonuses. The bonus for fifteen stars is sometimes as much as $75,000. Not bad!

What happens with a lot of my clients is they choose people to mentor based on the next bonus they are trying to earn. So, their primary focus is helping their people to go diamond, which puts more stars next to their rank. Repeatedly, I have people tell me they are investing their time in the people who are closest to achieving diamond rank, or people who once were diamond and have fallen off. Mathematically, it makes sense to help the person who is closest to the rank. And if someone has achieved that rank before, helping that individual get back should be really easy.

The problem with that? Sometimes these are people who are no longer showing up for practice. We are assuming their current worth to the team based on last year's stats. I don't care if someone ran 300 touchdowns last season; if they haven't showed up for practice this year, they aren't really a part of the team. Of course, they're welcome back at any time. But why would I chase them all over the planet, if I can't get them to show up for practice? Why would I draw up a play for a player who won't be at the game?

Wouldn't I be better off to work with the team that is going to show up? Let me just say this one more time, loud and clear: Those who are close to a rank or who have achieved it before are ALWAYS welcome back on the team. But they earn their spot the same way everyone else does: by showing up for practice.

So here's what I need you to do. Take another look at your downline. While you may want to keep using words like *team* for the sake of making everyone feel like a participant, you need to change your personal perspective of what that actually means from a leadership perspective. You have to ask yourself who needs you as their coach, and who may just need you to give them a stadium to escape to on Sunday afternoons after a tough week of work.

Joining your "team" doesn't mean they actually want to play. It may just mean they want to join the fan club or become a cheerleader. They may want to sit on the sideline and ride the bus. But you don't have the time or energy to have every single person, who really just wants to cheer, take over your bus or go out on the field to play.

The people who are showing up for practice consistently need you to show up for *them*. They need your time and energy. And while they may not be ready to score touchdowns yet, they have to be people who are willing to take practice seriously, listen to their coach, and put in the work it takes to, one day, score touchdowns!

CHAPTER 11

The Art of Asking Questions

Now that you understand who is on your team vs. who is in the stadium, I get to do the FUN part of this. You see, when you're working with the right people, leadership becomes very simple. I'm going to teach you a few things about mentoring people that you're not going to hear in very many places, because so few resources are being written specifically for the network-marketing industry.

When you are leading people who are technically their own bosses, who have no contract, and can do anything they want with their business, you have to learn different skills to mentor people. On one hand, it's a curse, because you have to work harder than you would in other industries to do the same thing. On the other hand, it's a blessing, because you're forced to learn new ways of doing things.

Law of Familiarity

When you are working with people in an industry that promotes community and friendship the way that network marketing does, all the lines can become very blurry. And that's why I'm so adamant about making sure you're working with people who are actually working, and not just anyone who happens to be in the stadium. But even the people who are working are often your friends or have become your close friends in the process. You may have been on events and retreats with them, and maybe even your spouses have become close. This is when you run into what I call the *law of familiarity*. It's my second law that I've coined. Nowhere near the hundred or so laws that J Max has coined, but I'm getting there!

The law of familiarity says that when two people become close friends, it makes it almost impossible for one to mentor the other. Another name I give it is *big-brother syndrome*. I'm the youngest in my family, and I've constantly defied anything my older brother has tried to tell me. Even at thirty-five, I'm like the little kid still trying to prove he's not the stupid little brother! I have three sons and one daughter, and my youngest son is the same way. If either of his older brothers tries to tell him anything, even when they're trying to be helpful, he immediately lashes out at them. "I KNOW WHAT I'M DOING!" he screams at them. His brothers tease him about being helpless, so he gets defensive and starts assuming that anything they say is questioning his ability to do something himself.

This is why you need to learn a new skill. And that skill is one of my favorite ones to teach. Its proper name would be *life coaching*, but to keep things simple, it's really just learning *the art of asking questions*. Life coaching is the single greatest skill I've learned in my time training under John Maxwell. It makes me sad to see how many leadership and motivation books there are, and yet, how few address true coaching. I'm actually in the process of creating my own PUSH Coach certification that will include life coaching, as well as all the training and mentoring resources I've learned and created myself. The training will equip leaders in the network-marketing industry to train their teams, while also creating career opportunities for people in other industries who want to get into the coaching field.

The skill of coaching, or asking questions, gives you the ability to help others find the problem themselves (and you don't have to be the bad guy). I've found, over and over, that when people determine the problem themselves and admit it out of their own mouths, they are a hundred times more open to actually receiving help.

The problem is that we, as mentors, too often try to call out people on their problems, which causes them to get defensive. Then they don't want to listen to anything we have to say. That is why it's so frustrating when a guest comes and speaks on a call for you, says all the same stuff you say, and then everyone thinks that person is amazing! Guest speakers don't have the law of familiarity working against them. But you don't have to have it working against you, either—if you know what you're doing.

When we ask questions, we remove the pressure. We show we're not accusing, but trying to help. Fortunately, it also keeps us from assuming we know the problem before it comes to surface. As mentors, our greatest weakness is taking for granted we know what others are going through. To some degree, we do. We've been there, in the same place, and we remember what got us out. And because we care about people so much, we're usually quick to tell them exactly how we got out of that situation. The problem is they didn't come to you so they could listen; they came to you because they need to talk, and they *need you to listen.*

There's no way you have time to listen to everyone like this. And so, you need to be careful not to mentor the wrong people. For someone who is showing up and working hard, I want to listen so I can help that person feel loved and move forward. However, if you are mentoring people who aren't doing work, and just want to talk about their problems, then you are no longer a mentor, you are a therapist. (FYI: You should probably write that down.)

The thing you're going to need to do is shut up. I used to keep a Post-it note on my computer with just LISTEN written on it to remind me to shut up and let others talk. It goes against our human

137

nature to listen when we know the answer. We were taught to speak up when we have the answer, not sit quietly, so we have to retrain ourselves if we really want to help others.

Beyond the Story

Once again, please remember this: *Our limiting beliefs are constantly looking for a story to justify our fears and excuses.* If we think that only "pretty people" succeed, we'll go looking for all the prettiest people in the company, follow them, and watch *all* their stories just so we can convince ourselves that our story is true. You need to remember this, as a mentor, because your people will rarely come to you with their real problem. Instead they'll come with *their story*. If you aren't careful, you'll end up "mentoring" them on a problem they don't have. But if you take the time to listen to their story, their subconscious mind will start leaking out the real problem to you.

There's a Scripture in the Bible that says, "Out of the overflow of the heart man speaks." This just means that if you let people talk long enough, what's really in their heart will eventually come out. The first few minutes is just head, emotion, fear. But if they keep talking, they'll begin to share their heart and their soul with you. That's where you need to get to!

Here's a paraphrased conversation I had with a listener on my podcast (Your PUSH Coach):

Josh: What can I help you with?

Bianca: I've been with my company about five years. At the beginning, I didn't really do much. About two years in, I finally started to believe in it and go for it. I've really been doing this for three years, and every single year, I've set the same goal and failed at it. So, my question is how do I find the motivation to keep going for the same goal when I've failed at it so many times.

Josh: You've been doing this for three years actually focused
and putting in effort?

Bianca: Yes.

Josh: In that first year that you were actually pushing for
goals, what did that year look like in rank and income in
comparison to this last year?

Bianca: Well, if you want to put it that way, I've made a lot of
progress. Maybe I didn't hit the goals I was aiming for, but
I've hit a lot of other goals in the process.

Josh: Can you give me specifics of the kind of money you were
making at the end of that first year compared to now?

Bianca: In the first year, I was making between $100 to $200
per month. Now I'm making around $5,000 each month.

Josh: Wait a sec, can you say that again?

Bianca: (Now laughing) About $5,000!

Josh: So, in three years of being a complete failure, the only
thing you've figured out how to do is multiply your
income by fifty!

Bianca: I suppose, if you put it that way!

By asking questions, I was able to help Bianca see that she is *not*
a failure, and that reaching for the same goal, three years in a row,
has got her what she *really* wanted, which was a full-time income.
She would be crazy not to go for that same goal again, because even
three more years of "failing" at that goal would probably land her
somewhere around $10K to $20K a month!

But I was only able to help her to see this by asking questions.
Questions allowed her to tell the story out loud, where she could hear
how silly her narrative sounded. I could've told her the answer from
the beginning. I could've said, "Bianca, the point of the goal isn't
to reach it, it's to stretch you. So, if you feel you've grown at all in
the last three years, you should keep setting the goal." Or I could've

said, "Bianca, it's not how many times you fall, it's how many times you get back up." None of this motivational crap would've helped her as much as letting her talk it out.

When you start to ask more questions, you'll start to see that people are a lot smarter than we give them credit for. Of course, like any art, it takes time to really get comfortable with it and for it to become natural. If you really want a good study of some live coaching, take some time and go listen to my podcast on iTunes or Spotify. About half the episodes are real life-coaching sessions, where I let you listen to how I coach others.

But you also need to dig in and just do it until it is comfortable. You need to practice getting on calls and asking people questions. When I teach this in my leadership groups, I'll usually give them an assignment to schedule three calls with people they're mentoring and make themselves use questions during the call. Every single time, they come back amazed at how powerful the mentoring session was.

Asking questions is also the best way we can raise up leaders instead of followers. Our whole lives, we've been taught that the leaders stand up front and teach while the crowd sits and listens. We're taught that what's written on the board is fact, and anything else is false. No wonder we have an entire society of followers. No one can even get dressed without checking Pinterest to see how someone else dressed today. When we ask questions, we force people to do something society has never taught them: We teach them to think for themselves.

Teaching Them to Fish

One of the greatest skills of any leader is problem solving. Leaders are responsible for so many different people, tasks, and responsibilities. One thing is for sure, you will have a hard time as a leader if you don't know how to solve problems. When we ask questions, we teach people how to solve problems by thinking for themselves. This will train them, over time, to start hearing your voice and your questions in their own heads. There will come a time when they won't need you to ask the questions anymore.

On that day, you'll have someone who has truly matured, as this person begins to take the initiative to ask the right questions. That's when you'll have someone who can go really far. Self-coaching is one of the hardest things to develop because it takes the emotional maturity to be able to look logically at your own emotional issues. It manifests when you are self-aware enough to be honest about your own shortcomings.

Asking questions is how we show others that we care. It's how show them that we're here to help them, not to control them. We have to remember that everyone subconsciously knows you have something to gain from them. They know that you make more money when they work hard, make sales, and recruit people. So even if you're the nicest person in the world, there's something in them that wants to rebel. There's something in them that wants to believe that you're "The Man," and that they should stick it to you. But when you ask questions, you remove that pressure. You release the defense mechanism and allow them to just talk.

Take a quiet moment and imagine being able to sit down with someone who has absolutely no skin in the game at all. Someone who genuinely wants what is best for you, whether it benefits or hurt them. Imagine how comfortable you'd feel talking to this person. Imagine how open you would be with this person. Now imagine being that person for your team. Imagine being the person they come to when they have struggles, instead of the person they avoid. Imagine people wanting to get on the phone with you to talk things through instead of taking two months off from their business without saying a single thing. That's the person you can become—if you'll take the time to listen.

You can create a safe space for your team, but you can also use this to help your friends and family. I try very hard, when friends come to me about life-changing situations, to use this skill to ask them questions so they can find out what they really want out of the situation, instead of me just telling them what I think they should do.

Now imagine raising up a team full of listeners. Imagine when you've properly trained your people to do the same for others. And over time you have a culture of leaders, because you have a team full of people who were forced to think for themselves. You have a team flowing with new ideas and strategies because of the creativity that erupts from these listening sessions! Imagine a team that no longer depends on *your* energy and effort because they've learned to work and grow without you! That is a beautiful day!

Remember that everyone has everything they'll ever need in life already living on the inside. Our job as a mentor is to simply draw that out of them. If we try to do too much, we may actually stunt their growth and hold them back from solutions that are more powerful than anything we have to offer. You don't need to fix people. You don't need to save people. You just need to believe in them, and trust that they have *their own magic* living inside.

CHAPTER 12

Mentoring Made Easy

One of the more rare skills I see in entrepreneurs—one that is actually a *vital skill*—is the ability to turn principles into systems. Something that bothers me more than anything about other coaches and trainers in my industry? Their lack of attention to helping others turn their principles into systems. One of the things I've specialized in for the last four years is taking the principles others are teaching and turning them into systems. Because businesses are not grown on principles alone, they are built on systems.

Systems make it easy for anyone to take advantage of the principles. But I've seen person after person read all the principles in the world, and still fail, because they don't know how to implement them. Memorizing J Max's *21 Laws* is cool, but knowing how to apply them will make you a lot more money.

Principles of Mentorship—Implementation

Let's talk about how easy it is to take the principles of mentorship and turn them into a system. We need a system that makes sure we are spending our time with our starting lineup, instead of the fans in the crowd. It doesn't mean we forget about the fans, and we definitely don't undervalue them, but we realize they don't need the kind of attention that our star players do. So, here are the factors I use to create a system that separates the players from the fans, and then turns my players into all-stars!

- Work with the working
- Hold proper expectations
- Develop a specific game plan
- Establish a way to track that plan
- Reinforce accountability: Reward for doing it. Create consequences for not doing it.

Work with the Working

As I talked about previously, we have to make sure we are working with the working. If you can't show up for practice, there's no way in the world I can coach you to be an all-star. But I need a way to find out who actually shows up for work. If you are mentoring people online, there's really no way of knowing what people are or aren't doing. Usually, we think the hardest workers are people who post daily, comment on team threads, and show up at events. I would agree that most people who work will also be doing those things. But that doesn't mean that everyone who is doing those things is also working. In fact, many of them aren't. You need to create some type of *team challenge* that will show you who is showing up and who isn't. In other words, you need to have a tryout.

I recommend taking everyone who is showing up for team activities and sending them an invite to join your new mentorship group. We won't tell them it's a tryout; we'll just let them know what is involved so we can find out whether or not it's something they want to do. A thirty-day challenge is about right. Enough time to find out if people really show up or if they just get excited about new things. We know from studies that it takes approximately twenty-one days to create a habit, so we need at least that long to find out whether this is something that actually becomes a habit in their lives.

Hold Proper Expectations

Then we make sure and set proper expectations for each person we're inviting. We want people to know exactly what they're agreeing to. We don't want to trick people into showing up for a party, when in reality we are trying to find out how hard they work. To be fair, people should know exactly what they're agreeing to.

Develop a Specific Game Plan

This is where the specific game plan comes in. Put together a list of everything you **need** your people to do on a **day-to-day basis**. I highly encourage you to start with what some companies call the *vital behaviors*.

The Vital Behaviors

   ◆   Be a product of the product.
   ◆   Invite people to join you.
   ◆   Engage in personal development.

Of course, you can make this more complex depending on the level of people you are working with and the goals you are helping them push for, but it should *always include* at least those three things. Some companies provide a specific tracker, and you can always use that if you'd like. I have one I use for my groups that tracks the following activities: plan out your day; write down your goals, affirmations, personal development; post on social media; start twenty new conversations; invite ten people to try your products/join your team; track your conversations and invites. It's pretty intense, but that's what I believe it takes to really succeed! But I would also dumb it down, if I were working with brand-new people.

Establish a Way to Track That Plan

Next, we need a way to track that specific plan. If we don't make people *prove* their level of activity, they will constantly give themselves the benefit of the doubt and think they are working harder than they are. I choose to use a digital tracker that makes their activities public to myself and everyone else in the group. There is no hiding in my mentorship groups! When you have people actually tracking activities in a way where it's public and they can't escape, they'll be blown away at how much work they've never done before! They'll also finally realize why they aren't successful.

Tracking the Plan

And now we need a system to reward those who stick to the program and to weed out those who don't. This is where people get stuck. Everyone loves to reward, but weed people out? That sounds like confrontation! But it's really not—if we set the rules and expectations in advance.

In my groups, I have my assistant calculate everyone's numbers on Sunday, and anyone who falls below 85 percent of their activities gets called out in a post on Monday. They have forty-eight hours to make up the activities or lose their spot in the group that they paid for.

But we also reward people. Each week on the live call, I pick a few people to give a shout-out to for performing well, or even for showing up on a week where they had a lot of personal trials. And then, at the end of the month, I pick two rock stars. One of these spots goes to the person who recruited the most people, and one goes to the person who recruited the most people in comparison to the month before.

It's important to reward both kinds of people. Your top performers should always get rewarded, because that's how you keep our best players around. It also creates social credibility for people to see someone else succeeding. But I also believe it's just as important to reward the person who's had the biggest transformation in their business, even if not turning in the best performance.

I want people to see that growing from 1 to 5 is just as valuable as already being at 10. Because growing from 1 to 5 is the way you eventually get to 10. And most of your people are at a 1, which means you need to show them there is a path to 10, and that you will always recognize them for taking the path, not just for arriving at the destination.

Let's wrap it up by showing you an example of the message you would send.

Hi Jessica! Hope you're having an amazing day!

I wanted to hit you up with some SUPER exciting news! I'm going to do a special challenge for anyone who wants to participate. I know that so many guys/gals on the team have huge goals and just need a little help to get there. I'd love to give some extra time and attention to people who want it, as long as you're down to meet me in the middle!

Let me know if you'd be interested in something like this, and I'll shoot you the details to see if it's something you're ready to commit to!

If they agree, here's message two:

I'm SOOO excited!!! I knew you'd be in!!!

So, here's what the group would look like. We'll have a call together every week when I'll share some motivation and tips, as well as answer questions you bring with you. This will give you a smaller group to get real about some stuff you need help with, but also give you a chance to reset your energy and mind-set each week.

We'll also have a tracker that everyone in the group will be expected to live by. If I don't know what activities, you are/aren't doing, it's impossible for me to help you make tweaks. I'll include a copy of the tracker so you can take a peek. It may seem a little intimidating at first, but just remember I'll be along for the ride and will help you to make it happen—as long as you're willing to put in the work!

Each week, we'll have a call-out post to hold everyone accountable to the tracker. If you fall below 85 percent of the activities, you'll get tagged in a post. You'll then have 48 hours to make up the activities or lose your spot in the group. This is intense, but trust me it's the accountability we ALL need if we're really going to go to the next level.

But I'll also have rewards to CELEBRATE people who stick it out! Each week, we'll recognize a few people who are seeing results or even just rocking their tracker in the middle of hard times going on in life! And then, at the end of the month, I'll reward two people with something really cool!!! The person who gets the biggest numbers will be one of the winners cuz, hey, it would suck to be the biggest performer and get nothing. But I'll also be choosing one person as a winner who's our biggest "transformation" story!!! This will be someone who saw the biggest amount of growth in their business over our 30 days together.

I'm sooooo excited about this group! It may seem a little scary, but I KNOW you can do this if you really want to! I just need to know, after seeing this, are you still in? Can you make a full commitment to rocking this with me? If not, let me say in advance that you are NOT letting me down. I created this group for you and the team, not for me. If it's right for you, then let's gooooo!! And if it's not, no worries. We still have the team page, team calls, and all kinds of stuff to help you grow until you are ready for something like this.

That's it! We just ask people to join us, let them know what's involved, and go from there. Some will join you, some won't. And let me just warn you in advance, for every ten that join you, there may be only two or three that actually stick with the group, and that's okay, too. We were never trying to turn everyone into a player; we just wanted to find out who the players are. From there, we keep the group going for those who stick it out to get ongoing access, and for the others to get another shot if they decide they are ready.

But this allows us to start spending more time with the people who really deserve it, and also have a place that creates an expectation of what being on the team is really like. It will force people to fish or cut bait! Except we're not necessarily trying to get people to cut bait. We're not kicking people out of the stadium just because they don't want to play in the game. We're just not going to give them their own locker and spot on the sideline either.

Go Forth and Mentor

Congrats, you are now ready to be a mentor! It's not as hard as you've been making it. I probably just saved you several hours per week. Because in one call per week, you can mentor the people *who matter.* If you have a larger team, I highly suggest having one of these groups for every major rank advance you are trying to help people reach. Instead of inviting the whole team, you simply have a push for first rank group, push for second rank group, push for third rand group, etc.

For the first rank, it might be a larger group that doesn't get quite the same level of your attention as in the other groups. And the trackers might be different for each group. But either way, you're taking the equivalent of many hours spent in 1:1 calls and accomplishing the same thing in a one-hour, (or less, if you want) group-mentorship call. But keep in mind: If you are mentoring people without trackers, you are wasting several hours talking to people who aren't doing anything.

The other great thing about these groups is that they partner people with others in a community of common energy, common goals, and common struggles! You'll find the community is a much stronger asset than your personal presence ever was. Even though people would rather have your personal time, what they really *need* is a community so that they don't begin to depend on you.

SECTION FOUR

MULTIPLY

CHAPTER 13

Empowering Your Leaders

"Josh, my team won't take responsibility. I've told them what to do over and over, and they just won't do it. I'm the only person posting in my team page. I'm so tired of being alone at the top."

Sound familiar? This is something I hear so many times. And I immediately know there is one of two problems:

- They don't have enough people for anyone to be involved yet.
- They haven't learned how to empower people properly.

Speaking Up

We live in a world that is raising up followers. In school, the teacher stands at the front and gives directions. The teacher makes the schedule for the day. The teacher tells you when do to what subject, when it's okay to talk, and when you should listen. For the most part, society has taught us that there is one leader in the room and the rest of us are supposed to sit and listen. If we speak up, have our own ideas, or question what it is happening, we are considered rebellious.

I met up with a touring artist one night for drinks after his show. He is a painter who has also illustrated some books, including a thirty-day prayer book that I have. He does some pretty unorthodox stuff, which is why I fell in love with him and had to buy him a drink.

If you want to see some awesome work that inspires you, challenges you, and sometimes offends you, you should definitely check out @ scottthepainter on IG. His show that night was amazing! He found a way to put together quotes, his own art, eighties movies, and storytelling into a presentation meant to deter people from suicide. It was one of the best presentations I've seen in my life.

As we sat in an Irish pub, we talked about what religion really means and things we'd love to see changed. One of the ideas that came out of the night was having people sit in a circle at church services instead of the typical theater arrangement. Having someone on stage tells our subconscious mind that someone is in charge and it's our job to listen, not participate.

I want you to think about this concept for a minute. Our whole life, we've been in settings where the person in charge is in front, and everyone else faces front. This alone says that one person is more important than the rest. One person has the answers, the rest of us are there to learn, not to contribute.

Now try to imagine why it is so challenging to get people to contribute. Our whole life, in almost every environment we've been a part of, we have been considered a part of the "crowd" in one way or another. I'll never forget one of the first leadership workshops I did for a church. I honestly didn't know what I was doing, but the training I had gone through taught me to jump and grow my wings on the way down! I came up with some specific things to teach on, and then made up a few interactive exercises. On the way to the event, I almost removed the interactive part of the presentation because I was afraid it would be cheesy. I was a little insecure about what I had to offer so I didn't want to screw it up. But then, I remembered that the only way to learn is to fail, and I wouldn't know whether it worked unless I tried it. So, I just went for it!

After the workshop was done, I handed out pieces of paper and asked everyone these simple questions:

1. What was your favorite part of the workshop?
2. What was your least favorite part of the workshop?
3. What's something else I could've done to make the workshop more effective?
4. Would you recommend this workshop to someone else?

I took some time right after the workshop to look over the papers. Of course, my insecurities were screaming, and I just wanted to see how I did. More than 90 percent of the group said their favorite part of the workshop was the interactive exercises. And more than half the participants answered number three by saying they wish there would have been more interactive exercises. The thing I was afraid of the most was what people loved the most.

What did this tell me about people? People love to be involved! The problem: We don't always create a structure that encourages involvement. It's one thing to tell people, "Post in the page anytime you want. I want you to participate." It's another thing to actually set the engagement up. When I have Q&A calls, sometimes it's like pulling teeth to get anyone to speak up. But if I actually call on someone, that person has a question almost every time. As leaders, we need to provide enough structure for people to lean on so they will be able to find their voices, moving past the social conditioning that restrains them from speaking up.

Breaking Out

How do you fix this problem? I hope by now you've learned that every problem we have is solved by *intentionality* over time. There's no better way to create intentionality than using a SYSTEM. Systems solve everything! We have way too many things on our plates to think we can just do something because we need to. My girlfriend and I have a scheduled date night *every* Thursday. We know that life is busy. We know that between my coaching business, her therapy practice, my kids, and life happening, regular date nights won't happen unless they're scheduled. In other words, we have a system for our date night.

So, are you ready to learn how simple it is to *multiply* when you have a specific system?

Lead and Contribute: Start with the people you're working with in your mentoring group. Those are the people you've decided deserve most of your attention, so it only makes sense that they are the ones you should be empowering and multiplying yourself into, right? Tell them that part of becoming the best version of themselves is to learn how to lead and contribute. They may not have a very large team yet, so getting involved with helping you lead your team will give them opportunities to learn and grow.

You need to ask yourself what these people are good at. Maybe a few of them are solid with posting. Maybe a few have great energy and are good on video. Maybe some are masters of organizing. Whatever the skill, simply assign each of them a day of the week and a category; then, schedule them to do their thing in the team page on that day.

You do *not* say, "I'd like you to post when you have a good idea." That will never happen. How do they know whether it's a good idea? They're not that confident yet. You tell them specifically something like this:

Jessica, you are AMAZING with posting on social media! Like legit, your posts pump me up EVERY TIME! I want to give you a chance to develop your leadership skills, which I think you and the whole team will benefit from.

Will you start posting every Tuesday in the team page, giving some posting tips? You could simply share the post you made for the day, and then give a tip or two on why you posted like that and how others could use it as guideline for their own posts. And then, just challenge people to comment below with their own post for the day, so we can go in and encourage them for their efforts! What do you think?

Of course, you could simply make it a part of the agreement of being in the mentorship group. And then, make assignments outlining the following: their day to post, what to post about, and what is expected. Now all of a sudden, you are not alone at the top. You have other people posting, which means you have other people growing in their leadership. You are also teaching them how simple it is to empower others. But maybe the most important thing you're doing is showing the TEAM that there are multiple people involved and doing things! You are giving yourself social credibility with your team. There is nothing worse than being the only one posting and engaged. As you learned from the law of energy, when no one is participating, no one *wants* to participate. But if you can get even a few people involved, that makes others want to jump in, too.

Value Many Perspectives: The other thing increasing the level of participation does is give the team the opportunity to learn from more perspectives. While you might be capable of teaching everything they need to learn, there are many things that aren't necessarily your strengths. Rotating different people allows the team to always be learning from those actually teaching from their strengths and passion zones.

If you're like me, you have learned to be organized for the sake of your business, but it is your least favorite topic to teach! Or you might be the opposite of me. Maybe you love giving organizational tips, but you *hate* teaching sales and recruiting. Now your team can see that there are different types of people with different types of strengths who are all finding a way to get results.

If you are the only one talking, people start to assume they have to look like you, sound like you, and be like you in order to succeed. And while you might be attracting your tribe, remember you're also attracting a bunch of people who *want* to be like you, not just people who *are* actually like you.

Empower Your Customers: If you are someone that runs groups or challenges for your customers, this is also a great way to empower your customers in a way that turns them from customers to business builders! If you already have customers that are super loyal and adding value, but not quite ready to join the team, why not ask them whether they want to participate in helping you run the group?

Sometimes people aren't ready for the responsibility of a title like *ambassador*, *rep*, or *coach*, but in their hearts, they really want to serve and pay it forward. This is a great way of finding out who really wants to serve. If they don't have a desire to serve, they're probably not a good fit for your team anyway.

Preach What You Practice: The next thing that you need to do is to simply teach what you're doing. If you have a mentorship group of people who are growing businesses, ask them what their next step is. Some of them may need to just focus on modeling. If this is their first time working on modeling, that might be enough to keep them busy for now. But if they've been modeling for a while, and now are starting to build a team, make sure they are either running their own Motivation Challenge, or bringing their people along for the one you're running.

Just make sure you get them involved with helping to run the Motivation Challenge if they're going to be adding to the number of participants with their people. Their people need to see them as leaders and influencers, and participating as a leader in the group will make sure that happens. If they are running a Motivation Challenge and have some of their team members really running and ready for more, get them running their own Mentorship Group with the same system I taught you in earlier chapters. If they only have a few people, and you don't know if they're ready to run a mentorship group, invite them to join yours.

One of my mentors taught me a really powerful process called **I Do, We Do, You Do**. The point of the process is that we don't send people out to do things alone the first time. That's not leadership. Leadership is being willing to *show* people what a process looks like first, then *invite* them to participate, and *then*, *send* them to do it. Never be afraid of allowing your people to help you lead for a short time before they run off to do it themselves.

Managing Capacity

Mentorship Groups aren't as effective if the group gets too big. So if adding people two levels down makes the group too big, feel free to run a few groups to keep the numbers ideal. And there's no magical number. I know from my own experience that anything over ten to twelve people gets exhausting. But I'm also someone who works with 1:1 clients daily, runs groups for hundreds, manages a five-figure per month business (sometimes six figures), and has a lot on my plate.

Your business isn't my business. Maybe you have more people or maybe you have less. It's up to you to ultimately decide how many people YOU want in the group, and how many groups you can manage. Maybe that means you have to make rules like "You can bring your own people into the group for two months, and then, you have to branch out and do your own" or "You're allowed to bring up to two people, but after that, you have to start your own."

Maybe it means you decide to work only with your personal recruits. Whatever it is, just make sure that everyone in the group is *held to the same standards*.

"But Josh, reaching into my downline just cripples my personal recruits. If I lead for them, they'll never learn." You're right. If you lead FOR them, they'll never grow. But let's talk about three scenarios that make it very dangerous to never reach into your downline:

Scenario One: Your personal recruit Danielle recruits Mallory. Danielle is working hard and seeing some results, but she's still struggling quite a bit with her confidence. Meanwhile, she has a friend, Mallory, who she works with that is really interested and wants to sign up under someone she trusts. Mallory is a FIREBALL! Like this gal gets it from day one! Her business takes off immediately, and she quickly surpasses Danielle by quite a bit.

While Danielle is happy to help her, she doesn't really have much to offer someone who has already outgrown her. Tell me, why in the world, would you pass up on helping someone that could be your downline's next rock star just because she's two levels down? Are you really helping either of them by refusing to help? In this situation, you'd be helping Mallory, who really needs a higher-level leader on her side to keep growing, and also helping Danielle, whose income *and* confidence could really explode if Mallory keeps growing.

Scenario Two: You have a guy named Matt (I had to use at least one dude example) that you've recruited, who is really crushing it! The biggest problem he is having is getting his team going. He has two recruits, Brittany and Jake, that are both showing up and doing their thing, just not seeing the results yet. It's getting harder and harder for them to keep showing up without seeing any results, especially since it seems like Matt is the only one seeing any success at all. Every week that they show up without seeing the kind of results they want is more and more proof that this business only works for some people.

What if Matt were able to bring Brittany and Jake into your group where there are ten other people who are working hard? In your group, you have two or three people who are seeing great results. Not only do these two or three people give Brittany and Jake hope that it really does work for everyone, but the two newbies also get connected with the other seven people in your group, who are also showing up in spite of the struggle.

As a result, Brittany and Jake have the ability to join forces with a much stronger community than what Matt had to offer. They make friends with people with whom they have more in common, and ultimately are able to stick it out and get results because of these new connections.

Scenario Three: I'll keep this one simple. Megan signs up with Tiffany. Megan is a badass who is willing to work and wants to do this! Tiffany sucks. She sits around collecting a check for Megan's work, but refuses to do anything herself. You and Megan both wish Tiffany would just quit. She's not doing anything to earn her paycheck, and it feels unfair that you could be rank advancing and Megan could be a part of something bigger, if Tiffany would just get out of the way.

Remember this: You can't control what Tiffany does or doesn't do. But Megan is still a person you are getting paid for. SO, HELP HER!!!! If you need to make some special rules that allow people like this to also take part in special prizes and trips you do, PLEASE DO IT! It is a slap in Megan's face every time she sees others rewarded and she's not included because she signed up under a dud that you are technically responsible for. It's a terrible representation of your company, and your company is probably too big to know it's happening or how to deal with it. So be a leader and deal with it yourself! You can't make Tiffany quit (although I might send her a nice/not-so-nice message), but you can take care of Megan.

Keep in mind that when only one person is succeeding, it's really hard for anyone else to believe it's possible. The more we can group people together with other success stories, and even others who are finding ways to keep showing up and working hard, the more chances we give people to succeed. Sometimes reaching down is actually the most empowering thing you can do for your direct line.

We just have to remember: I DO, WE DO, YOU DO! We don't let people use us, ongoing, without ever getting them involved. We use our intuition to decide how long people need before they're ready to go out on their own. But we also, and this is *so **important***, *get them involved with helping out anytime they are bringing their people along*. The only exception would be for someone like Megan. We don't want Tiffany to come along, and we definitely don't want her involved in leading! We just treat Megan as an adopted child that we treat as our own.

Spending Time with the Right People

Multiplying really is the simplest thing in the world. But this is true when, and only when, you are *mentoring the right people*. If there's one thing you walk away with from this book, I sincerely hope it's understanding how important it is to be spending time with the right people.

I get it, you want to see results and sometimes that makes us rush into wanting to help everyone. But if you can just remember that you have an entire football stadium to fill, and only eleven players allowed on the field, it will help you to keep laser-focused on the importance of avoiding distractions. You cannot afford to be thrown off by drunk fans that keep you from continuing to pursue finding your *players*.

Leadership sounds like the fun part. You want to get on calls and hang with your tribe. But every hour you spend on calls pretending you have a tribe, when you don't, is an hour you could've been spending finding your actual tribe! When you find your real tribe, you'll know it. They'll be the people whose blood runs cold when reminded of your tracker, but they stick with it anyways. They'll be the people who have no idea whether they have what it takes to lead, but they go start a Motivational Challenge anyways because they want to find out. They are terrified of mentoring people, but because they trust you, they just go for it. They jump and grow their wings on the way down! THOSE are your people!

CHAPTER 14

Continual Growth—Additional Streams

Soon, day-to-day motivation wanes. They begin feeling restrained or unfulfilled. They start focusing on protecting their success instead of progressing. Nothing seems thrilling anymore.

—Brendon Burchard, *High Performance Habits*

I hope that this book has completely shifted your mind-set about what it means to be a leader. From leading by example, to learning how to motivate and mentor others properly. But I would be absolutely remiss if I didn't write a chapter on the importance of **outsourcing** and **delegating**.

What I'm about to teach you has not only completely transformed my own business, but has given me the freedom to accomplish more in less time. I have the freedom to check out in the evenings without worrying about my business falling behind. I have the ability to travel and know that my business is growing even while I'm stuck in airplane mode. Most importantly, I have the choice to spend my time doing the things in my business that I most love and enjoy. Less desirable tasks—the things that exhaust me and drain my energy—are all done for me by my team and/or systems/funnels we've created or paid someone else to create for us.

Life by Design

Imagine for a minute waking up and spending your time not only with people who "fill your cup" (as I taught in the mentorship chapters), but also on activities and tasks that fill your cup. Your life literally becomes "life by design." It's sad to me how many people claim they have life by design, when what they really mean is that they make a lot of money working all the time. Sure, they can work from anywhere, but what if they want to actually be present with their family somewhere? Working on a beach sounds like the dream-life, but what if they want to actually swim in the water?

True life by design means that you can choose to work or choose to not work, and you still get paid. While you're reading this, I have assistants responding to messages for me. I have ads on Facebook, Instagram, and even third-party apps that are putting people in my inbox, where my bot is delivering them free ebooks and then getting them to take surveys to help them discover the root issues of why they're struggling. To which, of course, my assistant is then responding by reaching out with scripts I've created to point them to the training that can help them.

I want to walk you through a typical day in my life. I wake up around 7:20 a.m. to get my kids up and ready for school. I fill out my Self Journal while the kids are getting ready. I drive my middle boy to his private school, while my dad takes the other two boys to their school. My little girl then stays with him for the day, while I work. Because I am *not* a morning person, I go back home and take a little nap. My reward for doing my journal and getting the kids off to school is getting to catch a few more z's before my day needs to begin.

Around nine o'clock, I take my pre-workout, make my daily post on social media, and workout. I have a call with one of my 1:1

clients at ten. Sometimes I have one more call at eleven. Then I do my affirmations while I'm taking a shower and getting ready. I head to a coffee shop nearby if I'm on a tight schedule, or downtown if I have a few hours. I listen to an audiobook on the way. When I get there, I pull out my to-do list. Right now, my to-do list is made up of six simple tasks: Journal (which I've already done), Personal Development (did it in the car), Writing, Add Value, Promote Current Event, Make a Sale.

I have around two to three hours to write for my book, do something that adds value (usually an email to my list or running some type of motivational ad to my followers), do something to promote my upcoming event, and get creative about making a sale. Sometimes I'll add a call to action in my email, sometimes I'll post in my groups about some type of promo I have going. But even "Making a Sale" usually consists of me creating some type of call to action that one of my assistants can then go respond to and close the sale. My job is to create the content that starts the conversation, not to actually have the entire conversation.

While I'm doing my to-do list, I have anywhere from six to ten different ads working for me and two team members talking to people, organizing my groups, and responding to my emails. Now, after reading that, tell me if you really have "life by design" or if you just have "work all the time."

I'm going to go ahead and call you out on your BS before you have a chance to think about it. Some of you are afraid of outsourcing and delegating your business because you have the opposite problem of one I discussed in the Model section. Your problem is not that you struggle to model, your problem is that your ego has you so attached and addicted to modeling that you do it just for the sake of wearing a hard-work badge on your girl scout uniform! If we're being honest, you are working so hard that you are exhausted, your family doesn't get the best of you like they should, and you're not even all that excited about what you do anymore. But you're afraid that if you let go of anything, (1) people won't respect you anymore, and/or (2) other people and systems won't do as good a job as you would.

Let's address both of those. If the only reason you work so hard is to keep people's respect, you're doing this for the wrong reason. The point of starting your business was probably to create a better life for your family and to inspire others to do the same. Let me ask you this: Is working all day and night giving your family a better life? And are you really inspiring anyone by working so hard that you're missing out on life itself? Do you really think anyone wants to be the next version of you, if that's the life you're creating?

I do believe that, at the beginning, there are some sacrifices you have to make to get things off the ground. But you need to be honest enough to realize when that season has run its course and you can now transition into another season. Don't ruin your family or mental health in the name of leading by example. Instead, be smart enough to continue modeling *without trying to do it alone*.

Delegating

Just because I believe in modeling the right behaviors, doesn't mean I think that you should do it all yourself, when you can afford to get help. What is more important is having the emotional and creative *capacity* to chase the next thing that can help you reach even more people, so that you can teach the people who are ready for it how to go to that level with you. Not everyone is ready for that next thing. But if you don't learn it, you can't teach it to the people who are.

This year alone, I've launched a new podcast, am working on a PUSH Coach certification, have a live event I'm putting on and promoting, and am working on a new book. All things that still give me the ability to wear my hard-work badge, but also things that will move this business to a new level. And the truth of it is these things would not even be possible if the rest of the business weren't delegated and outsourced.

It doesn't make me a phony; it means I care enough about my own health, my own family, and everyone reading this book to pass along things I don't have to do, so that I can do more of the things that only I can do. I love what John Maxwell says about this topic—that if someone else can do something 80 percent as well as you, than you shouldn't be doing it.

The other problem people have is thinking that no one else can do it as well as them. Again, I call BS! First of all, a lot of the things you're doing are copy-and-paste activities. In other words, you're literally copy and pasting scripts that you've typed up, or you're doing something you've done a thousand times, so it's no longer genuine anyways, just a repeat of the other times. Like creating groups, sending welcome emails, sending multiple messages that say the same thing to check in on customers or follow up on potential clients. All of these are things that a monkey could be doing for you, and yet you choose to hold onto rote tasks pretending you do them best.

The beauty of hiring someone else to do things for you is they don't have an entire business to run like you do. They can actually accomplish things twice as fast as you can because they don't have as many things on their mind as you do. They're not thinking about the next post they need to make, getting another five stories up before bed, the goal they need to hit by the end of the week. They have the task list that you gave them to do, and that's it! They can crank through those activities like they're nothing. Not to mention they won't overthink every activity like you do and end up spending way too much time doing something that can't be done wrong in the first place.

One last thing you're thinking is that it costs too much. For some of you reading this, you make plenty of money; but for others, your money may still be paying the bills. Here's what I want to ask you: If I were to give you just five extra hours a week, do you feel you could make one extra sale?

When I hired my first assistant (my older sis, Lish, who is still working with me and a vital part of our team), I told her I could give her only five hours a week to start, and that if it went well, there may be more hours down the road. She was more than happy to make any extra money at the time, and five hours per week was a great way for her to start, too, because she had no idea whether she was even going to like the work.

There are one of two approaches you can take from here. One approach is to hand off things you can train someone else to do that make sales, to be sure your investment pays itself back. So, if you have something you particularly dislike doing that leads to sales, like sending scripted follow-up messages or even scripted new-conversation messages, you can hand off these things. Or you can even ask yourself if there's something you're constantly dropping the ball on that would make you extra money if you were to start doing it consistently. Once again, train and delegate.

Leveraging Your Time and Talents

The other approach, which is what I did, is to give them things to do that take you the most time because they are outside of your strength zone. For me, sales and talking to people are among my greatest strengths. I knew hands down that if I had more time to message people, do consultations, and speak on calls, I could increase sales.

So, I had Lish doing the things that took me the most time, which were processing sales, sending welcome emails, and setting up all of my Facebook groups that I used for monthly training groups.

Even though completing these tasks took her five hours, these same activities could take me up to ten hours to get done, simply because they were so far out of my strength zone. I always put off working on them, and when I finally did, I hated the process so much that I found myself scrolling the news feed instead of completing them. When Lish took over these simple things, I had ten extra hours to focus on sales!

In the first week, I took on extra consultations, signed on more clients, and made back at least 10X what I was paying to have my first team member. We don't use the word *employee* because it's icky, and I don't want to provide "jobs" for people; I want to give people their own business that they can be proud of! So all of my "employees" are independent contractors with their own businesses. They set their own hours, just like me. As long as they get things done, I don't ask at what hour it was done, or if they were in an office or a hot tub when they did it! And that's why we call ourselves Team Legacy (my LLC is Legacy Leadership).

I've worked to create a "WE culture" that empowers all of the team to have input in how we do things and even create their own systems for how their job gets done. I partner with really good people who believe in the mission of this company, and then I trust them to do their job *better* than I could do it myself. It doesn't mean I never check in. It just means that I empower them to be badasses, and then, expect that from them! When I do have to call them out, which happens very rarely, they take ownership and fix it right away. But they also have permission to call me out! They let me know when I haven't done something I said I was going to do, and they probably hold me more accountable than I hold them.

Today, Lish works for me full-time, as does my good friend, Josh Ring. J Ring, as we call him, actually has strengths very similar to mine. Since Lish can handle all the office work, J Ring acts more as an extension of myself. He focuses on managing all my Facebook groups to make sure the energy is high and that people are getting taken care of when they have questions and concerns. He also does a *lot* of behind-the-scenes sales. We make the perfect team!

Having him doing sales in the inbox allows me to focus on continually creating new content such as posts, emails, and ads that get people responding. For a few years in my business, I had moved away from trying to get people in my inbox and focused more on sending them to my website. There was just no way I could possibly keep up with talking to every person interested in signing up for a course. But no matter how incredible your sales page is, people always have questions you didn't think to answer. Even more importantly, people need affirmation they're making the right decision.

I can't tell you how many times someone has gone to my website, read the information about my groups, then asked me to clarify the difference between one group and another. I legit copy and paste what my website says. "Thanks so much, that really cleared it up for me," is the response I get *every time*!

Sometimes people just need to know there is an actual human on the other side of the transaction. So, having J Ring in my inboxes frees me up to spend more time creating posts and emails that get people TALKING to us, instead of just trying to send them to a sales page. He knows my groups in and out and even gets on the live calls so that he can hear my language and know exactly what I'm selling and what the training courses include. When someone asks a question he doesn't have an answer for, he sends it my way and I shoot him a response. He then saves my answer so he knows how to respond the next time.

Without Lish and J Ring, I would still be working with ten to fifteen 1:1 clients and running one training group that would max out around fifty to a hundred people. And I definitely wouldn't have time to be writing this book, creating a PUSH Coach certification, hosting a podcast, or enjoying as much of life as I do. They make it possible for me to actually work with fewer 1:1 clients, but charge more per person, as well as have groups with capacity for unlimited numbers of people (hello, residual income). I have time to create more content to sell, and I have the capacity to travel and speak more in person, which always leads to more sales.

Outsourcing

In addition to having my own team, I also outsource some of my social media ads work, the growth of my Instagram account (I still create the content), biweekly cleaning of my house, the oversight and production of my podcast, and basically anything else we need done that doesn't fit into my team's strengths or schedules. This may be hard for some of you to imagine, but as your business grows you have to constantly protect your time and energy. You have to ask over and over, "Is the investment of time and energy into this task worth the payoff I'll get in return?"

If I'm speaking on a call, it's going to take up to an hour of my time, but it will also promote my brand and message, deliver some immediate customers, and drive others to my social media pages who will eventually turn into customers. That's worth my time! Even if only one person signs up immediately, I made $200 for an hour of doing what I love. That's not the best pay off, but considering that person could end up doing my group for two to three months and then sign up for additional events and trainings, that one customer is usually worth $1000 to me. That's a $1000 transaction that only took me one hour to create.

If I'm going to make a graphic I know will end up taking an hour or two, I have to keep in mind that the graphic itself does not sell my group or create money. And I could outsource that graphic for $10 to $20. So, for every hour of creating graphics that could be outsourced at $10 to $20, I can potentially speak an extra hour for $1000. That's a great trade off!

Now, my mind will try to trick me and point out that I'm not going to speak *every* hour when I outsource a task. But then, I remind myself that I have a physical, mental, spiritual, and emotional capacity. While outsourcing a task may not lead directly to me speaking on a $1000 call, it conserves my physical, mental, spiritual, and emotional resources to take an opportunity when it does come up. It also protects my capacity to make sure I can deliver the best of me each time I am showing up for any of my calls. It ensures I have the energy to create good content. It guarantees I have the capacity to bring my full energy where it matters. Not everything has a direct impact on your income, but everything that has a direct impact on your *energy* has an indirect impact on your income.

If you're someone who wants to **continue multiplying**, remember that you will have to continue modeling, motivating, and mentoring. But you don't have to do it by yourself! Outsourcing gives you the ability to reach more people, while still protecting your personal boundaries and making sure you're continuing to enjoy your business. I don't believe you have to be a martyr in the name of success or making a difference. I believe that only selfish people do that.

But that's just the payoff from the original customer. For every thirty to forty people on a call, 20 to 30 percent of them will follow me and see posts and advertising for future events and offers. I estimate that around 10 percent eventually become customers. As I mentioned, each customer is worth about $1000 in lifetime sales, with the occasional person that becomes a 1:1 and is worth $10,000 plus.

Life Is More Than Work

If you choose to be married to your work, it's probably because you're avoiding something else in your life that you don't feel in control of. Maybe you have a bad relationship with your significant other (been there). Maybe you have a child who is going through a rough time and giving you hell (been there). Maybe you are just afraid to slow down and listen because you may hear something you don't want to hear (definitely been there).

Please remember that your work is NOT your life. But if it's something you love, it can be an incredible part of your life! It can be something that gives you joy and fulfillment, while also giving you the freedom to make incredible memories and contributions with the people you love and care about the most. This entire book was written to help create the boundaries you need to do that.

This book has become my conviction. Because I see so many people stuck in so many different places. I receive dozens of surveys, every single day, from people who are struggling, and 98 percent of those people answer that they are working four-plus hours a day and making less than $1000 per month. That breaks my heart!

I work with people in my PUSH Leader group who admit, when they join, that they have no idea how to motivate and mentor their team. That they feel "all over the place" and absolutely exhausted. My 1:1 clients come to me, so many times, as people who are so successful and yet so run down. Success has kicked their ass! While they have incredible paychecks, many of them making more per month than the average American makes in a year, they have arrived there by working themselves to death. They don't know how to streamline their business and systems, and haven't outsourced as much as they should. After the opening call, they have hope because of my laying out the Four Ms for them and explaining how simple this approach really is. They see that there is a way to navigate, continuing to grow while also helping their team grow. If you are someone who has given up your personal life to create success, and are ready to make some serious changes, I have a very special survey for you at https://joshcoats.com/survey. The Outsource and Automate Survey will help you to find out if you are ready for the next step in your business. You will find that through automation you can actually scale your business to the next level while spending less time on your business and more time enjoying your freedom!

Wherever you may be stuck, I hope this book has given you clarity and hope. Without clarity, there is little hope. But with clarity comes a breath of fresh air. I hope and pray that you will take these principles and put them into practice. You don't have to do everything I've taught; you just need to abide by the simple principles. And you need to remember to take it one step at a time. You don't need to multiply today. You need to model today. You need to motivate, with no strings attached, and trust that the right people will be ready to come under your mentoring wings soon!

And then, you must embrace those you have to mentor, no matter how few. You have to be willing to fail. But please, above everything, remember this: It's better to have failed others because you gave something insufficient, than it is to have something that you never even gave. If you do nothing for others, you fail by default. But if you fail in the process of trying, you learn *valuable lessons* that you can pass on to others.

I believe in *servant leadership*. I believe in making the world a better place. But I also believe that the only way to really serve others is to be honest with them about what success really is, and what it isn't. That starts with being honest with ourselves. It's time to take your mantle back up. It's time to RISE and become the leader you were called to be! It's time to let your fire shine so brightly that people fill the stadium to watch you burn! It's time to be everything you were born to be. It's time to do everything you were born to do. I believe you were born for such a time as this. Now rise up and take your place!

About the Author

Josh Coats lives in Tulsa, OK, with his beautiful girlfriend, Jenny, and his four kids, Dakotah, Kaiden, Paxton, and Amaiah.

Josh is a high-energy, no-excuses, no-BS motivational speaker and business coach. He is a certified life coach, but more commonly goes by PUSH Coach to create immediate urgency and expectation from his clients.

After making only two sales his first year as a life coach, he took his business to social media where he found his niche in working with network marketers. As he learned the structure and terminology of network marketing, he began to specialize in putting personal development and leadership into terms and systems that network marketers could easily understand and apply. He hustled his way to making over $48K part-time in year two, and then grew to six figures in his first year of doing it full-time.

His bestselling training, The Art of Recruiting, has trained more than 5,000 reps. He hosts monthly webinars with 1000 plus in attendance, and travels around the country speaking for events and retreats. He has personally mentored over a dozen reps who were top ten in their companies and built up a waiting list of over 100 to work with him 1:1.

Josh is the author of *Clarity and Focus for Entrepreneurs* and host of Your PUSH Coach, a podcast for network marketers that takes you behind the curtain with 1:1 coaching sessions to help you to identify and overcome your limiting beliefs.

He also trains other life coaches on how to take their businesses from zero to $10,000/month, and is raising up a PUSH Team of other PUSH Coaches to train and mentor people in all industries.

When Josh isn't speaking on calls, you'll find him working in a local coffee shop, watching superhero movies with his kids, or at one of his favorite cocktail bars downtown.

You can follow his daily journey on IG https://www.instagram.com/joshcoats_pushcoach/or on FB https://www.facebook.com/joshcoatspushcoach/. To subscribe to his free monthly trainings or to join one of his virtual business boot camps you can go to joshcoats.com. Make sure and check out Josh's 5 Day Recruiting Challenge to kick start your mindset and strategy for taking your business to the next level! Get started for just $38 at https://joshcoats.com/product/five-day-recruiting-challenge/

For survey links and link resources:
joshcoats.com/survey/

Acknowledgments

This book is dedicated to the millions of humans that are out there hustling to build their dreams and make this world a better place. More specifically, to the network-marketing industry that has welcomed me with open arms, trusted me in team trainings and events, and shared me with their friends and colleagues.

I know how hard you work to serve your social media followers, customers, teams, and families. I pray this book will give you a clear system to help you serve all of them without losing what is most important to you! I want you to have all of the success in the world, while making a difference in the world, and still having time to spend with the people you love! You can have success without losing your peace of mind.